A MAN

WITH

NO NAME

KENNY LONE EAGLE

PAGE PUBLISHING, INC.
Conneaut Lake, PA

First originally published by Page Publishing 2021

ISBN 978-1-6624-1063-5 (pbk)
ISBN 978-1-6624-4220-9 (hc)
ISBN 978-1-6624-1064-2 (digital)

Printed in the United States of America

PREFACE

I am now at the age of sixty-six I have written this book to show young and old that through adversity and hard times, we can make it in this world. I am a born-again Christian. I have always been different from anyone in my family. I have learned at a very young age that determination and persistence will help you make it through hard times in life. There is a God; he has spoken to me two times in my life. If he had not been watching over me, I would have never survived it this life. This book is full of challenges that I have lived through. One must be extremely observant and learn from others' mistakes.

Growing up, we all make mistakes, but the lesson is to tell yourself I will never do that again. I made it through this journey by learning manners, respect, and honesty and finding friends who are a little smarter than me to help make decisions and older people to help guide me. I was raised to think that white people are smarter than us of color. Back as a child, many would treat me as an uneducated boy. That made me determined to learn proper language skills so when I interacted with them, they would soon realize I am not an underclass human. Born with a last name of Flores, many thought I was a Mexican, and I got in many fights with racist kids who bullied me.

My dad wanted us to go back to the name of Eagle, but he was not a person of determination. He did, however, have a naming ceremony in 1989 where he gave me a name change which is now Kenny Lone Eagle. Although this book is full of eyebrow-raising situations, I have witnessed in my life was good between these stories. The God of Abraham has given me all the things I have needed in life which included two beautiful daughters, Stayce Lynn and Kimberly Marie, and three grandsons, one of which I raised as my son due to hard times with one of my daughters. His name is Kenny Mathew Eagle. I also have a daughter from my second wife named Kimberly Ann whom I also love.

The reason for me writing such a detailed true story is because so many children have been abused and cast to the side with no support. To those kids, remember you are loved, maybe not in your present situation but there are good people. Your ship is out there, but you have to swim out and pull it in! There is no shortcut in life. You have to set your goals high and be patient; nothing is instant. Picture life as a big whiteboard with a few dots on it. These are your connections you will have throughout life. As you meet people and become friends by earning their trust, you get more dots and those dots know other dots. Some dots are large and some small, but they are your connections; you need these connections to help you when you need help. One dot is a mechanic, another a carpenter, another a banker, and so on, but it is up to you to earn their trust. I hope this book will help someone. God bless.

I n 1953, a boy was born. The furthest back my memory goes back is to the day when my two sisters, my brother, and I were left alone in a one-room, very old apartment in Terre Haute, Indiana. I was about four years old, maybe a bit younger. My birth mother and my dad had divorced, and she moved us four kids there. She was dating a man named Frank and had been leaving us children alone in the apartment for sometimes days at a time. There was little to eat, and she made friends with a lady across the hall and asked her to check in on us once in a while. We had nothing, and my dad drove down from Gary, Indiana, to bring us a little TV.

When he got there, he quickly saw the situation and was furious! Someone must have sent word to her wherever she and her boyfriend were, and they showed up. My dad was a very connected man in the Syndicate. A form of the mob in Gary. I remember him taking the other man in the hall and setting things straight! He said, "I am taking these kids, and if you come after them, you may not come back," and he meant it. Next thing I remember was holding the wooden rail in the back side of the apartment walking down the stairs. The rail was high for me to reach because I was very small. I remember sitting in the back seat behind the driver's side and was too small to see out the window, but I looked up, and it was an overcast day. This is my life story, Kenny Lone Eagle. All accounts are as close as I can remember. I was always different than anyone else, and little did I know God was going to use me in one of the greatest life lessons He was to put on me more than most anyone because he had work for me.

Although many either kill themselves or wind up in prison because of their childhood, I was the opposite. Born to a Native American and a Caucasian woman, I was given all the traits and looks of my native ancestors—the dark eyes, hair, no body hair, and such. Now my great-grandmother, Julia Nieto, was pure. She was born in 1873 right smack in the Indian campaign out west. I have researched her as best I can, and her death certificate just says Indian as race. She had two boys and a daughter—Raymond, Joe, and Ines. Now my dad was a war hero who never spoke of the war. He signed up at the age of sixteen because he too was passed around and had a hard life. He did not know how to raise kids, so he depended on his half sisters. They were good women who had kids of their own and were good to us. Their daddy was Walter Holguin. As far as my dad's dad goes, he said he was an Indian alcoholic who died in the back alleys of Chicago.

Many times through my life, my brother and I would ask him about our grandfather, but he never changed the story. He did manage to keep my brother and I together as we were passed around though. The very first place I remember was getting dropped off at my aunt Alice's home; it was a plain weird pink brick-colored home in East Gary, Indiana, on State Street. We stayed there for a short time; her husband did not like us. I suppose we were a bother. Next, we moved across the street to my aunt Lillian's house again on State Street. We did not stay there too long because she got into a butcher-knife fight with a lady named Emma over Emma messing with her husband. Aunt Lilly was in serious condition and was really sliced up bad. I saw the wounds and bandages. God knows how many stitches she had. Next, my grandmother took us in. She and her husband, Walter, had adopted a boy our age, and he was the nephew of Walter. We was told we were cousins, but that was not true. My grandmothers family did not treat us the same as some of the others, but I was not able to understand. I just had that instinctive feeling something was not quite right even as a little boy.

Now Walter pretty much spoke Spanish, but he was white. Later in life, I found out he was of some German descent. He was a very strict man, and we had to go to his church where he preached in Spanish. Not knowing the language, it was a torture, but he meant well. This had me confused even as a child. He and his family tried to tell us we were Mexican, but I had this strange feeling something was weird because my daddy did not speak Spanish and I just could not connect with the culture. Also, they all treated this cousin we lived with different than us. They called him Sonny, but his real name was Hector. We got along fine.

While living there, I saw this reel-to-reel tape player in my grandma's daughter's room, and I was curious, so I was looking at the reel, and it fell to the ground, rolling all the tapes off! I did not know what to do because it was an accident. She came home and put me in the shower, turned on the water, and beat me almost out of my mind with a rubber shower hose! All I remember hearing was my grandmother screaming at her to quit. It did something to me mentally! From that moment on, I was very careful on what I said and thought out everything that could happen to me if I made a choice that could be bad for me. Later on, things began to change when I finally started getting educated when my grandmother told my brother and I we were Indians. Wow! This was interesting! So we listened to what she was about to teach us.

As she lay in bed, we would sit on the bed and she would tell us stories, but she said, "The things I teach you? Never tell Papa!" That's what they all called Walter. She said he told her that now that she is married to him, she is no longer an Indian; she is a Mexican, and he forbid her from teaching his kids the ancestry. But my brother and I could not get enough. She showed us how the ladies dance and how the women stroke their hair one hundred times in the morning and one hundred times in the evening and many other stories. Now I was beginning to see things differently and, even as a child, putting things together. So it was in the summer of 1959 when Grandma died. I remember this green ambulance parked in the yard and saw her on the gurney. I was six and remember that day clear. I never saw my dad cry, but that day destroyed him. I just kept to myself and got out of the way. Well, from there, it was home number four. Aunt Sally took my brother Mike and me in and my sister Michelle.

The tiny home was as close to dirt floors as it gets. She was a good lady. I loved her, and she treated everyone the same. Her husband's name was Frank Olivary. I stayed clear of him because he was mean, and I did not want anything to do with that! He was always yelling at her and would use what was called a razor belt on the kids if they made him mad. One night, my dad showed up in serious condition He had been stabbed and had a jar of acid thrown at him. His back was almost to the shoulder bone because he spun around as the gangster threw a mason jar of acid at his face. Again, I saw the damages on his back and the knife hole. He had a blue-and-white 1950 station wagon, and he slept in it.

There was an old man a few houses away named George Earl who would give us kids a piece of candy now and then, and right next door was the Pavy family. All the people living in the area were low-budget. Some would say we were poor. But a child does not know they are poor. They only know this is a way of life. One time, my aunt told us if we go out and work really hard and dig worms, we could sell them and she would take us to this big amusement park called River View. Wow! We were excited! We worked all summer, and she kept all the money in a can. We finally had enough! That is, until her husband found the can and went to the bar and drank it all up. This really hurt us, and we all cried. By this time in life, I was really learning how to deal with disappointment. Rich Pavy next door was older than my brother and me, and he told my brother if he did not eat a worm, he would throw a spider on him

My brother ate the worm because he was afraid of spiders. I was still too young for school, but Aunt Sally would make a homemade biscuit with butter on it for my sister and brother for school lunch. We never had toys, so we made our own. Aunt Sally showed us how to make a kite with newspaper and using flour with water to make glue for the string that went around the edges. They flew pretty good. Time to move again. Aunt sally's family kept growing. She wound up with twelve kids, and her husband divorced her, leaving her with no money and all these kids. That made me angry, and I never wanted anything to do with the creep!

Well, we moved in a little tiny one-room apartment with our aunt Lilly; she was living in Gary, Indiana, on the poor side of town on Washington Street. We learned that when the milk truck was delivering that we could steal a quart of milk. We were always hungry, and that cold milk was a real treat! We decided to run away from that place because it was basically in the slums of Gary. So we just started walking. I know for a fact that God was watching us because we were in a dangerous part of town and had no idea where we were going. All we knew was we were going to try and find our dad. We went in a tavern called Bachelors Tavern and asked the people at the bar if they knew of a man named Mike Flores. As luck would have it, believe it or not, he was staying in a room upstairs. So he took us with him.

During the day, Dad had to work, and an alcoholic friend whom they called the Professor was watching us off and on during the day. He took us to the Coney Island for lunch to have a hot dog and bowl of chili. He died of alcoholism. So then we went to live with a friend of dad's named Big Jean. She was a nice person. Little did we know we were living in a whorehouse. She did a good job keeping us unaware of what was going on, and her house was very clean. For the first time in my life, I actually had breakfast, lunch, and supper. She made sure we had clean pajamas and a clean bed and even tucked us in at night. Upstairs, Indian Pat lived. She was a whore who was a sweet person. Whenever there was a John or a customer, Big Jean put a watch on our wrist and gave us a quarter to down the street to the store and come back in a half hour. Indian Pat also died while we were living there. She overdosed on drugs. The street we lived on was Jackson Street.

Time to move again. This time, it was a nightmare! My second cousin Arthur and his wife took us in because they were living upstairs of my uncle Ray's house and needed the money my dad was paying. I was in the second grade and went to Miller School. Miller was on the outskirts of Gary, Indiana. We lived on Decalb Street. Me my brother and sister Michelle lived there. We were forced to eat for supper every day a can of peas with an egg cracked in it. To this day, I will not eat that! Also, all our other food was government cheese and Spam, along with beans. He used to accuse her of cheating with the neighbor, and they would get in bloody fights; he would beat her and grab me and say, "You better tell me!" And then she would grab me with her bloody face and say, "You better keep your mouth shut, you little son of a bitch!" I was scared to death!

Every night, they would watch TV and eat New Era potato chips and a cold bottle of Pepsi, but we were not allowed to have any. If we made them mad, they would lock us in this dark scary attic and tell us this is where the which lived and she will get us! Sometimes we had to pop the pimples on his wife's back or maybe in the evening pick the dead callous meat from the bottom of his feet. He used to walk everywhere because he did not have a car. There were times, out of the blue, she would say, "All right! You kids get outside!" We had no idea what was to be.

Then she said, "Start fighting!" We did not want to fight because we loved each other. But she said we could not stop until someone draws blood! Many times, I had to lie there with my brother crying and saying close your eyes so he could punch me in the mouth to draw blood. I was so mentally messed up that I could not spell Pepsi. They would punish me because my brain would lock up and could not spell it out of fear. He was really into watching baseball, and he would force my brother and I to pick a team, but we knew nothing about the game! So we would pick one and could not stay up long enough to watch the end. If we lost he would punch us in the arm, and if we won, we got to hit him. But how hard can a seven-year-old hit?

Many times, out of a dead sleep, he would snatch me up and hit me so hard my entire arm would go numb and I would cry. There was a nice nonviolent boy across the street named Window. She would see him out in his yard and tell my brother go out there and kick his ass! My brother did not want to hurt him, but she said, "I will beat your ass if you don't!" So my brother had to beat up this innocent kid. To this day, my brother has problems. Well, I failed the second grade, and as I was walking home, the more reality sat in. I was sad, then upset and looked at myself as a failure. Every step I took, the angrier I got at myself and then I said to myself, "They think I am stupid! They think I am not smart!"

Then I started punching myself out of anger and made my mind up that I will show them! I will show them all! So the next year at that same school, I made all As. I made a change in my life that day and became a different person.

From there, I moved downstairs with Uncle Ray. He was Chief Lone Eagle and taught me who I really was! He took my brother and me under his wing and showed us the Indian side and how to dance. My two cousins Rubin and Robert had a band called the Eagle Brothers, and this is where I learned about my music skills. They showed us the way. They used to dance until they got too old. Then Mike and I took their place. We used to dance in shows in Hammond, Indiana, and Chicago. There was an actor named Basil Heath, along with Iron Eyes Cody, who liked us and treated us good. Little did I know that later in life, Basil, also known as Chief White Eagle, would adopt me. Well, after we left that place, it was back to Papa's house on Green St., East Gary, Indiana. Walter took us back because no one wanted us. We slept on the floor with one blanket to share actually. It was no big deal; at least we had a place to sleep.

Again, he was a very strict man, and I kept my distance. My brother, sister, and cousin Sonny walked down to the main road and caught a bus to go a couple miles away to Gary to see a movie. They had a fun time. But when they got home, he took off his big leather belt and beat them severely! He said this is for going to the house of the devil! Again, I saw this and had my own backflashes. There was a kid just a little older than us named Alan Burley, and he was a mischievous kid. We all went to the local school just to play and hang out, and he picked up a rock and threw it at a school window! He laughed and said try it! I said no. My brother did it because Allen kept calling him chicken, and later I threw one. I did not like it because I knew we should not be doing it.

Well, a couple kids with the last name of Cargile turned us in. My dad paid for the windows but did not beat us. Thank God! Dad was not a child beater, but he did scold us for it. Next, we moved again, only this time it was in Papa's basement. There was this giant coal-burning furnace, and the truck would dump chunks of coal down the shoot close to where I slept. By this time, I learned how to cook eggs; it was that or go without, but I got really good at it. I was in the third grade and had this mean old lady teacher. I had forgotten to get my homework done, and she called me up there and hit the top of my little hand with a ruler so hard that it busted the veins and my entire hand was black on top! I had nobody to tell because no one cared about me.

By the third grade, I have been seeing all kinds of cool things. A kid brought in a Cox P51 Line control airplane that was chrome for show and tell I thought that was the coolest thing I ever saw, and it had a real motor in it! Also, my brother and older cousin joined the Boy Scouts, and I thought, *Wow!* They get to go camping and learn outdoor stuff too! Well, I lied about my age so I could join. Looking back, I think the scout leader knew I was too young, but he took me in. Well, I went to the Good Will in Gary and dug through the clothes and found a Boy Scout uniform! Woo-hoo! I put it on for my third-grade school picture. I was proud I finally got status! Oh well, time to move on again.

Oh, before I was moved, while I was living at Papa's house on Green Street in East Gary, one day, my dad stopped by and told us he was going to put my brother and me on a bus to go to visit my birth mom in Terre Haute. Actually, I did not remember who she was. So we went there, and she had married Frank Cox and had one little boy named Roger. I was totally mixed up, wondering who this child is that my mom had. He was white like his dad, and I was dark like my dad. So that mixed me up. I was probably eight or close to it by this time.

Her husband worked at a powder mill, and later it exploded, but he was not there when that happened. My mom seemed nice, but again, I did not fit in and felt like a stranger. By this time of my life, I became like a coyote—very cautious and careful with different people because I have learned that every family has their own rules, and they all had different foods they ate, and some were people with bad tempers. So I was very alert and kept my mouth shut. I suppose I was similar to the great Comanche warrior, Quanah Parker. Although his mother was white, he looked and took after his people. I was always different from others because, I guess, it was a way of survival. I had already been exposed to ways more than a little boy needed to witness.

While I was there, I saw my grandmother on my mom's side; her last name was Elrod. My grandpa was George Leon Elrod, but I never really knew them and only saw them a couple times in my life. All the family on my birth mother's side had nothing to do with us. I always thought it was because we were dark complexioned, so I kept my distance. So now I had another thing to figure out. The people who I thought were my direct blood relatives were actually my dad's half siblings of another man who chose the path of their dad, which was Mexican, even though he was white. They tried to convince me I was Mexican too even though I could not connect with the culture. Something just did not add up! The more I thought about it over the years, the more angry I got. I was determined to get answers even if it took all my life. So now here I am—a little boy who felt not accepted by the white side of the family and was not part of the family my grandmother had. I had no identity and did not know my real last name. I was about to become someday, a man with no name!

Kenny Lone Eagle

My dad's last name was Flores, which meant wild-flower in the native, but he never knew his dad, and Grandma could not read and was blind from diabetes who had other children throughout her life using a midwife to birth them and had a few daughters who did not survive. When it came time for my dad to go to school, my grandma grabbed the wrong birth certificate and registered dad as Margaret Flores. He got in a lot of fights over that. It was not until he got older and got the name right his name was Mike E. Flores. The he said stood for Eagle. He was not raised with my grandmother; he was raised by Chief Lone Eagle. This is where he got all his knowledge of our ancestry, along with Grandma Julia, who was born out West in 1873 right smack in the middle of the Indian wars. She was snuck across the border into Mexico to save her life. Her mother is unknown, and her death certificate says her race was Indian. You see, back then it did not matter what tribe Indian you were. If you were Indian that was it.

Okay, next home to be moved to was in East Gary, my dad's girlfriends home. Her name was Nancy. She lived with her mom and took my brother and me in as a favor because she was dating my dad. She was very mean to us, so again, I was careful around her and her family. Again, I did not fit in. She had a son our age named Bobby, and we got along good. I liked Bobby. She would not allow us in the house, and we had no toys or anything to play with. She forced us to just eat cooked cabbage every night for supper. I was sick of cabbage and refused to eat it for many, many years. She made us go to bed at eight o'clock even though the sun was out in the summertime

That was torture for young boys, but she did not allow us in the front room, and if company came over, she would stick us in the basement, which had nothing down there. It was dead of winter, and she would not let my brother and me in the house. We had no winter coat and were freezing. I remember sitting on her porch stoop next to the house, cuddled up tight, hugging my brother, shivering to keep warm, but finally, eight o clock came and we got to go to bed. We tried to tell our dad, but he had nowhere else to take us at the time. One day, my dad came over her house in the evening to visit, and I was wanting to see my dad so bad, but again, she made us stay in the basement. I went up the basement stairs to just crack the door so I could only see him. I needed my daddy!

She saw me, then got up and snatched me by the collar and threw me all the way down the stairs! I remember slow-motion bouncing headfirst down to the bottom, then things went black. I was knocked out and broken up all because I wanted to just look at my dad. I heard later that my dad was angry at her over that and took us back to papa's house for a short time. This was to be the last time because Dad met this lady that he really liked and wanted to get married and try to start a new family life. He and her bought this little house with a slab floor in a subdivision in Miller, Indiana. It was the outskirts of Gary. So another move. We moved from papa's house to the Miller house. This was the first time I ever remember being with both of my sisters and brother all together. By this time in life, I was set in my ways. I was not a bad boy, but I was very streetwise and kept out of trouble. The lady Dad married was named Kitty. She treated us fair, and I loved her. She understood me. I was a chubby kid and was not obese, but stocky. Others used to cut me down, and she always took my side; she was a good stepmom.

Now I am in the fifth grade. Dad always had good intentions, but he was not raised by a dad, so he did not know how to be a dad. Dad had his own problems he had to deal with. For one, he would not allow our birth mother to have us because he knew she was not a good thing for us. Also, no one but me knows his war story because he would never tell anyone and he kept it to himself. He was in World War II at the age of sixteen and was awarded the Silver Star, one Purple Heart with three clusters, meaning he actually was awarded four Purple Hearts for spilling blood on the battlefield. He was shot by a rifle. They fixed him up, and back he went to have a hand grenade tossed at him. Then back he went only to be stabbed by a bayonets; they fixed that, and he went back to get crushed by a half-track after opening up a way through the enemy line to allow the Americans to break through. This is why he was awarded the Silver Star. Needless to say, he spent a lot of time in the bars.

Okay, so this was going to be the final move for a few years. One day, Dad and Kitty told us four kids when we were staying at the Aetna subdivision that he and my step-mom got married. Go figure! There was no wedding, but we took them for their word. It did not matter anyway because kids had no say so in anything back then. It was always, "Because I said so! And you never mind!" Well, they bought a bigger home, and we were all going to move there. This was the first time my oldest sister Toni Darlene, Michelle, Mike, and I actually all lived together. It was *great*! I always loved my siblings even though we were not always together. Toni was the oldest and very smart. She was our leader but if it was something we needed to all vote on to agree she would let us have our say. Next was Micky or Michelle. Micky had her problems, and it stemmed from being jumped around with other families.

She was also mistreated and used to be put in the dark attic at the one place where we were all beaten and witnessed many terrible things. Sister Toni did not see the things the three of us saw; she was with a better family. Brother Mike was messed up too and became one who always had friends around him who gave him support. I, on the other hand, was wise in my own way because it was a survival thing. I did not like getting hit and had a good memory. I was my own person who thought everything out. If I thought I might be doing something that may be wrong, I would ask myself, what is the worst thing that could happen to me if I got caught? If it was really bad, I would not want the consequences so that kept me out of trouble.

Well, we made the move to a subdivision in East Gary, Indiana. Part of Dad's plan was to get my stepmom's two girls that she could not raise. The oldest one was Linda Mcglaughfin, who was living in a children's home in Kouts, Indiana. She had lived there for quite a few years and was about to have a hard time readjusting her life with four other siblings that she never met and not known anything about us. My step mom Kitty had another daughter the same age as me, and she lived with a foster-care lady named Mrs. Ross. She too was about to get a major change in life with a family she knew nothing about.

Linda was smart at school, and Kathy the other sister was a good kid too. Although we had some serious clashes with them, it was because we were all from these mixed-up childhood prior to being put together. The house was, to us, a big home, but now looking back, it was not as big as it seemed although it had four rooms; the rooms were small. It was a newer home, a bi-level and was a nice home. The subdivision was named Old Orchard. Our address was 2017 Vigo St. There were new homes being built by L. M. Stensil. He was a contractor back then. I was in between the fourth and fifth grade, so I finished out the year at east-side school in the fourth. I was a boy who was all boy! I wanted to play baseball at lunch hour, but the other kids did not know me, so they would not pick me to play. The biggest boy's name was Kevin Popcorny. He was a big redheaded guy. Finally, they were short one day, and I got my chance, and I gave it my all! I became a regular, and I was happy.

One day, over the classroom's loud speaker came the announcement that president Kennedy was shot! We were all in shock! Killing a president was unheard-of! I still remember that day. The next thing I remember is, they had an announcement on the loud speaker that they were wanting to see if anyone wanted to be a patrol boy. Back then, the patrol boy was in charge of seeing that the kids got across the street safely. I asked for the job and got picked! Wow! I was important! I enjoyed having a little authority and wearing the special shoulder strap that distinguished a patrol boy. I felt a little out of place in this school because I was the only dark-complexioned kid in the school. Many times kids would ask me, "What are you?" Probably because I did not have broken-up English like maybe a Mexican kid would have. I spoke clear, fluent English because that's how I was taught.

Well, finally, guess who I met up with? The bully of the school! I was a nonviolent boy and, for sure, did not want to get paddled by the principal, so I was a good kid looking for no trouble. The bully's name was Ron Santell. All the kids were afraid of him, but I never met him until one day. It was during class break when we got to use the restroom, and I was at the urinal minding my own business when someone came up from behind and pushed me in it! All the other kids laughed at me, and I lost it! I shoved him as hard as I could! And he said, "Oh yeah? Meet me after school." And I said, "Okay, right after I get off patrol duty!" Well, that was the talk of the school: Kenny is going to fight Ron Santell! So it was here I am in the fourth grade and have no way out of this! I was afraid, so he said, "What is it? Do you want to wrestle or fist fight?" I said, "You choose!" He said wrestle. I had an adrenaline rush and lay on to him and had him down so fast that it was nothing! Wow! I thought he was going to be a handful. Come to find out he was just a bully who liked seeing kids afraid of him. Next day, I was the talk of the school, but I did not let it go to my head because I did not want trouble.

It was at that same time in the fourth grade while living on Vigo St. that I soon met this kid who was my age; he was a really skinny and small boy His name was Roger Gibson. They too had not lived there long, and he had no one to hang around with, so we started hanging out. We were on the same page in life, meaning we liked riding bikes, playing baseball, hunting, and camping. I was a free street kid. I had basically no rules, except stay out of trouble. Although I never lived much with my dad in the past, I figured he was nothing to mess around with. Roger and I met other boys near our age from other parts of the area. Roger had a sister named Barbara Elaine. She was in the second grade, I was in the fourth, and she had a crush on me. I did not know anything about girls or love, and she was missing all her front teeth and waiting on permanent ones to come in. She would just sit and watch us play sandlot baseball. We kids had nowhere to play, so we found a field, and all pitched in with lawn mowers and made our own. Back then, if you wanted something, you had to find a way to get it.

Although my dad worked in the steel mills, we did not have any money because he told me one time he made two hundred dollars a week. Being there were six kids and a stepmom with a drinking problem, along with all the bills and Dad going out with his buddies, playing cards and spending a lot at the bars. Well, figure it out. Again, all through my childhood, I had no toys unless I traded someone for them and cashed in pop bottles or milk jugs. Back then, a milk jug brought in fifteen cents. So mostly Roger and I spent almost every day in the woods behind the house.

We made our own traps and caught all kinds of stuff. One of our favorite was a figure-four dead fall made out of an orange crate and three sticks. One time, I caught five quail at a time! But mostly rabbits. My brother Mike and Roger's older brother hunted a lot too. Although Roger and I went our own way, Mike and Bruce set up a figure four of their own.

We did not have guns, so we shot everything with a bow and arrows that we bought at the local hardware. They used to sell cheap field-tip wooden arrows and darts too! The good darts with feathers on the back and a steel point. So one day, Mike and Bruce went to check their trap back in the woods, and it was sprung! Woo-hoo! It was evening time, and they were discussing who got to make the kill when they lifted the box. They agreed to flip a penny, head or tail, and brother Mike won! So he drew back the cheap fiberglass bow, and when the crate was lifted, it was a skunk! Mike was stunned for a second, and the skunk did not run. Instead, it turned around and sprayed both of them! Mike shot it and was proud of his kill. They carried this thing right through the middle of the subdivision! People were running, closing their doors.

Well, guess where the skunk ended up? In our house basement! Meanwhile, our dad was driving home with my oldest pregnant sister Toni, and two blocks from the house, my dad said, "Oh man, I smell a skunk." The closer he got home, he said, "Man! this thing must be close!" And he was! Right in his basement! Well, that's the first and only time I saw my brother get a beating, and he had to wash his clothes in tomato juice. Bruce came over later, and he and Mike were showing each other their whooping marks, and Bruce had Louisville slugger across his butt. We still, to this day, laugh about that. Needless to say, we did not bring home our game and backed off using the trap. I was getting in to the fifth grade, so Roger and I would ride bikes and wanted money, so we started cutting lawns so we could buy pop to take in our fort. Forts were a popular thing. We took a shovel and kept digging deep, then put a metal roof or whatever we could salvage. We would eat potato chips in there and hang out in the hot summer days.

One time, Mike was into forts and secret places too, so he found a spot under the staircase in our bi-level and took a wood-burning tool there, and he and I formed a club called the Eagles Club We knew we were part of the Eagle family because our dad told us that as long as I can remember. So he burned the Eagles Club on the staircase, and I believe it is still there today at 2017 Vigo St. It was in my fifth grade that I had a very mean teacher. He liked using that paddle! He would paddle girls too. His name was Mr. Kosinski. Being the way I was raised with some of the child abuse, I was on the top of my game! I was afraid of him every day because I just had a very bad feeling about this guy! He, to me, was just waiting for me to mess up, and I was smart enough to know it, but I could not let him know! I was a pretty sharp boy who could smell bad, and he was it.

Halfway through the school year in February, my mom was kind enough to bring cookies to the class. I was very nervous about that. But thank God in heaven, when she showed up, she recognized him from her school days. She said, "Stan?" He said yes. She said, "Stan Kozinski?" He said yes, and they knew each other! Wow! I was in shock. After that, he was nice to me, so I give God all the credit for that. The rest of that school year went good and my stomach problem got better. So around that time at home, Roger kept asking me to go to church. I only went to a Mexican church and knew nothing about church in a language I could understand. So finally, I went with the Gibson family. By then, their family was getting bigger, so we all piled in, and Mr. Gibson drove. Mr. Gibson's name was Thomas He was a very good Christian and provided for his family. He was a very strict man, but then again, he had to be in order to keep order. Mrs. Gibson cooked fried chicken every Sunday, and Roger would sneak me a piece or two. We did not think she knew, but she told me when I was much older that she cooked extra because she knew Roger was sneaking it to me. So I learned a little about Jesus and started going often.

One day, I wanted to go but overslept, and I was upset so I hitchhiked there. I had a wrinkled white shirt on because that's all I had, and a man stopped and said, "Where ya going?" I said, "I am hitchhiking to church because I missed my ride." This nice man drove me all the way. I was grateful. Out of all the people in our household, I was the only one who went to church, so my dad used to call me the black sheep of the family. Actually, he had it backward but did not know it. So I let him say it because it did not bother me. All of us boys in the neighborhood also played football; we had a lot of fun. Although our football had torn laces and the bladder hanging out, we still had fun; we even played with one that would not hold air.

On to the sixth grade. This was going to be a big step because we could change classes. Now I will be going to Edison Junior High School big-time. I had to walk to school about two miles each way but did not mind. I was in good shape because we played and ran a lot because we were never in the house. This year is about to bring trauma, and I did not know it.

Okay. So I started school, and we got to choose classes, and one of those was band or choir. I always wanted to play a saxophone in a rock band, so I thought band would fun. It was the first day of school, and my first class was going to be band class. I went in the room and was a good boy just looking at all the instruments and minding my own business. The other kids were all talking and having fun because the teacher was not there yet. His name was Mr. Greveti. He walked in the room and was a mean man who started yelling at the top of his voice, saying things like, "If you think you are going to have fun and games all the time, you are seriously mistaken!" He had a red angry look and I did not feel comfortable at all. Then he went on to say if anyone in here does not want to be here leave now! I thought, *Here is my chance to change my mind.* I walked out of his class, and he did not like it. So I joined choir and that was more peaceful. So It was not over. I had him for science class too! I knew I had to be a good kid. After all, I did walk out of his band class. One day, he came in the classroom and said he was going to be gone and there was going to be a substitute teacher, and if he hears of any trouble, we would pay! I knew he was another man who liked swatting kids, so I had my mind made that I would not give him any problems.

Well, on one of those days, a Friday to be exact, the teacher left the room and two stupid boys kept messing with each other. Bob and Bill were their names. It escalated to the point where one was chasing the other around the class. I saw this and put my head down on the desk because I wanted no part in that, especially after the threat from our teacher before he left. The substitute came in and saw this, ran out, and got the principal. Another paddle-happy guy to come down to our class. He pointed, "You! You! You! And me! Come to my office!" I told him I was innocent. He said I should have told, but I could not because she ran out soon as she saw the mischief! Well, he did not punish us, so I felt somewhat relived. The following Monday, this teacher came back and right away called us in to the hall and began yelling at us, I told him I had nothing to do with it! He gave me the hardest five swats I have ever had to this day over something I was totally innocent about!

That evening, I was still furious and told my dad, and he did not say anything! I felt like no one wants anything to do with me and will not support me even when I was done wrong. I had made my mind up! I will never take a swat for something I did not do ever again! If I am going to make it in this world, I had better handle it myself at all cost and that was final! Well, during that year, I was picked to serve on the student council. I thought that was fun, and the Beatles came out and the song wipe out was popular, so I wanted to get in a band because across the street from the school, there was an old church converted to a dance hall where kids could hang out on Fridays and listen to local bands. A lady named Mrs. Seeban ran it. I wanted to get a band and play there too because boys in a rock band was the big thing. Only one problem. I didn't have a guitar. And I didn't know how to pay one yet. So every Friday, I sat up by the band and stared at this guy's hand as he would chord his guitar to try and remember how to place my fingers.

One night, he said, "Do you want to learn?" I said yes, so he said, "I will show you one chord at a time. When you learn that, I will show you another." Wow! While they were on break he let me practice that one chord my fingers hurt, but he said they will get better. I don't remember how, but I landed a beat-up guitar and played the way he showed me, but it did not sound at all like his guitar. So the next week, I told him and he said, "Is it in tune?" I said, "What's that?" He laughed and showed me a simple way to tune it. Wow! I made a chord on my junk guitar, and it kind of sounded like his! Woo-hoo! The problem with mine was the strings were too high from the neck, but I just had to deal with it. As the summer went on, I kept learning chords one at a time. Then I learned the bar chord, and this is the one rock bands use a lot!

Finally I met a couple boys called the Bingham Brothers; one played lead and the other played bass, and they let me try out with them. They knew I needed some work, but they let me in, and I practiced every day! I finally traded for a Tasco electric guitar. It was low-budget, but it was all I could get. I got really smooth, and our band needed a name, so we called ourselves The Crustations. We finally got our chance to play at the teeny bop dance hall for kids, and I was on stage! I loved it! Bands were popping up everywhere. My brother had his band, and I had my band, and it seemed like everybody had a guitar and playing in garage bands. The neighborhood girls would just sit for hours listening to us practice. It was fun times. Roger and I still hung around, and we started going camping and fishing on this polluted river called Burns Ditch. We used to fish for carp. I was always the one who packed all the heavy gear, but we took eggs and bacon so we could cook on the campfire. I never told anyone we were going camping because no one cared enough to miss me.

We also packed a .22 rifle with about five bullets and hid it where we were camping in case some murderer would try and kill us; we hid it in a place where we knew where it was. We were very responsible boys and understood gun safety. But we always had a peaceful evening. One time, when we were hiking down the river, we found twelve-foot fishing boat. We came back the next day, and it was still in the same spot in the middle of nowhere. So we decided to claim it. We had to drag that thing for about four miles through the woods to get it home. I always wanted a go-cart, so one day, while riding bikes, we saw some kids working on a homemade go-cart, but I thought I could make it run, so I asked them if they might want to trade their go kart that won't run for my boat. They said sure! So I dragged my boat over there and traded, then dragged the broken go-cart home.

Well, the go-cart was a homemade job and had to be pushed home. My friend Roger and I pushed that thing for about a quarter mile to get it home. I had it in this one-car garage. Back then, only rich people had two car garages because most folks had only one family car. So I started tinkering with this thing. I was always intrigued by mechanical thing and wanted to see how they worked. I wasn't very knowledgeable but started trying to make it run. Before I knew it, one day, the garage door was open and a cop pulled up and started asking questions about where I got it and whose was it. I said it was mine. But he said it was reported stolen! Now I was only about maybe twelve years old at the time, but I said it was mine and I made a fair trade! He said what did you trade? I said I had a rowboat but didn't say anything else about it because I took it from the river. Well, he said, "Get in!" Then said, "Take me where you got it so we can straighten this thing out."

Well, we went there and came to find out the kids I traded had stolen the go-cart. So believe it or not! The police officer was kind enough to put my stolen boat on his car and bring it back home with me. Wow! I was sweating bullets! Now we weren't bad kids, but we had nothing and no one to teach us about life. My entire life was always about figuring it out for yourself, and if I got in serious trouble, I was on my own because my dad would not back me or my brother up. We were going to learn about life the hard way. A lot of my knowledge came from being very focused on what happened to other kids when they got caught, so I was very careful and learned quickly never tell on yourself and hope they do not figure it out. But if they did? Clam up and let them come up with a rational reason for me. Maybe they might go light on the punishment. My brother and I had no toys or games, but we weren't ever led to be violent troublemaking boys we were just 100 percent boys.

One day, my brother said he was at a house, and in the shed was a lot of board games that were just stacked up, so he convinced me to go with him and steal or borrow some. I was really scared because I was not a thief! Well, we broke in and took a couple and brought them home. We played them until we got tired of them and had to go back for more, but we always returned the ones we took, so we were friendly thieves. It was wrong, but that is how street kids think; in other words, if you want it, find a way to get it without hurting someone. As for my bike, it was made of a bunch of parts but always had good tires because there was usually someone from the neighborhood who went to the rich side of town and took a bike that was nice that some kid just left in the front yard. The kid would take what he needed and tell the other kids what was left, and then he would probably toss it in the river. They never kept the frame because it had numbers on it.

One time, during that age, my brother made some friends that were always known for being mischievous. My brother was a follower, and by being with these guys was part of their bad behavior. My brother Mike was not a violent boy either, but one time, those guys went down the street where some new homes were being built and shot out some windows in these houses. People kind of had their eye on us certain kids and would tell the police who they might want to talk to. Well, the cops came to our house and saw Mike and me outside and waved us over. Mike was one of those guys who was involved shooting the windows, so he said to me as we were walking, "Whatever you do, don't say *anything*!" So the officer was Mr. Orlich, and he looked at me and must have saw that I was nervous. He said, "What do you know about these windows down the block that were shot out with a BB gun?" I stood there and said I didn't know anything. He then looked at my brother Mike and said, "How about you?" He said, "Sir, I don't know about it either." The cop looked at me and said, "You're lying and you're going to jail!"

I said, "Mike did it!" My brother looked at me and said, "Kenny!" I said, "I ain't going to jail for you!" The cop started laughing; he was shocked how fast I came clean. Well, he said, "You and the other kids' parents are going to have to be contacted" and did not take us to jail. We still laugh about that today. While living at that same house, my buddy Roger, his older brother Bruce, Mike, and I were into the forts and other kids too, so we were rabbit hunting during the snow months with clubs. That's right, clubs. Bruce said we can track one down to maybe a log and scare it out and maybe have a chance. Believe it or not, we did just that and got one! It was a tall old grassy area that was let go and a two-story old abandoned house there.

Well, I was in the seventh grade and still had the old double-barrel. While at school, I met other kids who also hunted. One of them was a good friend and a really funny guy. I really liked him, and his name was Leroy Rice. His mom and dad were real Italian and good people. We used to go there and shoot at each other with rubber bands in their little front room and laugh. His dad was pretty accurate too! One day, we were playing and I got a lucky shot and stung his dad in the tip of his big nose. As he was bending over to pick up rubber bands he yelled, "My nose!" It turned red, and we laughed for quite a while over that. Well, Leroy and I used to go hunting for rabbits, but he also hunted with other kids that I didn't feel safe around. Again, I was always watching which way that muzzle was pointing and would quickly tell them if I saw it.

One day, Leroy went with some other kids, and the other kid was behind him, and somehow, the kid's shotgun went off! Maybe the safety was off. Anyway, he shot Leroy in the head and killed him! I was really torn up over this, and it was the most dramatic funeral I ever saw! His poor dad was crying, saying, "Oh, God! Why my son! Why not take me!" It was heart-wrenching to see this. Well, another lesson to make, just that be more vigilant while hunting. I was always a leader and did not trust many people for my safety through life. Well, back at home, my dad would let anyone live there. Of course, they had to fend for themselves as far as food, but they could live there. I stayed away all the time, except to sleep. I could have gone to California and no one would have missed me. My dad would say, "Just call if you leave so we know you're making it." I felt like I was not important and no one cared for me. I can count off the top of my head—my stepmom's aunt, her dad with the electric voice he used to talk with, her aunt Sis, her brother Butch, and five others.

I can't recall any Christmas gifts, maybe cologne or something. As matter of fact, my sister Michell's boyfriend Jim Cartwright said to me, "Hey, smell this cologne your sister gave me for Christmas." It was mine, but I didn't let him know she stole it from me because it was no big deal. One day, on Christmas day, I was sitting outside on the concrete steps, kind of feeling sorry for myself and thinking, *Well, another Christmas with nothing*, and a voice came in my head, saying, "Don't feel bad! When you get older, you will have all the toys you want!" And it happened! Today God had blessed me with the means to do just that! He has been watching me all this time and taught me how to turn every single bad thing that has ever happened to me upside down and use it for the good. He has put me through all this to mold me in to someone who can help and understand what others are going through. So instead of feeling sorry for myself, I decided to get more mentally tough! Life is a battle! And I am going to fight this mental battle! Well, God was there for me again because the next traumatic experience is right around the corner!

One Friday night, my neighbor friend named Paul Neglosky asked me if I wanted to go to the dance. It was a two-mile walk to get there, and I asked the lady who ran the place if our band could play there. She said yes, so we practiced about fifteen or so songs and was on the list. Paul had a girlfriend named Pam Tokash. I was alone, just hanging out, watching the girls dance. It was a big deal because I never seen so many girls my age, and they were all fixed up and pretty. I was afraid to ask one to dance for fear of getting turned down, so I just hung out and had fun watching the band. This was in the summertime, and I was just getting ready for the ninth grade. Paul's girlfriend, Pam, was going in the eighth grade. Pam was with her girlfriends Debbie Hallmark, Cyndi Moffatt, and Jo Ann Comstock. Paul told her he was no longer interested in her and broke up. Later that night, one of her girlfriends told me Pam liked me. Me? Why? I did not know her very well.

Anyway, we met and I thought no big deal. It was one of those things where junior high kids liked each other and nothing serious. I knew absolutely nothing about girls or how they think, but it felt good to know someone liked me, so I said okay. I like her too. It wasn't long before we were talking on the phone and slowly learning things about each other. We were getting along good, and it went on for quite a while. Then we started meeting up at the dance and we danced together. Pam was an average-looking girl, and that was good for me because I didn't have to worry about every guy trying to steal her from me. I was already insecure and did not want any more heartaches in my life. I was fifteen and did not have my permit to drive yet, so Pam would catch the bus and come over and visit me. She was only thirteen. Pam was my very first girlfriend, and it felt pretty good.

We stayed together, and I soon found that she trusted my decisions. I was very smart at life for my age and was not a troublemaker. The only serious fights I got into was because of someone mistaking me for a Mexican and bullying me. I usually won. Soon the word got out I was an Osage Indian and would fight back. They stopped picking on me. Pam had pretty brown eyes and pretty brown hair. She was a clean girl and cared about how she looked, and I really liked that about her. I respected her and was always there for her. I never raised a hand to her and put up with her moods. I started seeing these different mood changes but did not know anything about girls, so I heard that girls are sometimes moody so I'll just shut up and would let them pass, and they did.

One day, she and I were hanging out, and she said, "Have you ever passed out?" I said, "What do you mean?" She said, "Hold your breath until you pass out." I said no. She asked me to try it, so she said just hold your breath until you pass out. I was totally confused but said, "I will give it a try." We were dating about a year at this time, so

I held my breath until I started feeling this weird buzzing and dizziness. I stopped and said, "This is crazy. Don't do this!" I did not find out that she did this often until years later from her parents that she would do this when she was mad about something. Pam was a very sweet and caring girl with underlying disability's that she hid very well. She was a very sensitive and emotional girl, and I was sympathetic to what was ever bothering her. I was her rock.

We had the same dreams of someday having a log cabin with a pond and land. We were very close, and I loved her very much. She was the only woman I have ever been with. We went to church, and she was saved and baptized, and so was I. We both tried to be good Christians. One day, we were sitting in my junk car just hanging out, and I had this little Red Ryder BB gun across my lap. She was sitting in the driver's seat, and I had the barrel in my right hand. As I was putting BBs in the barrel, I was explaining gun safety to her and how never to point at what you don't plan to shoot. My right thumb was over the barrel hole while I was loading the BBs, and as I was teaching her—*pop!* I looked at her in shock and looked at my thumb, which was throbbing and saw a BB stuck in there! She started crying because she didn't know the gun was cocked and saw the BB in my thumb. I was cool about it and saw her crying because it was an accident and took out my pocketknife and dug it out. Lesson learned for both of us.

We were together every day. We were high school sweethearts. She would wear my football jersey at the games and was always there for me. Pam was very sensitive and could get her feelings hurt easily. If she was hurt, she would not respond until later. Then cry. She and I smoked cigarettes because that's what everyone else did back in the day. We drank beer on the weekends to socialize too because that is what we thought we were supposed to do also. We grew up together and stayed together married for thirty-five years.

Well, as I wrote, us kids were rabbit hunting by this old abandoned two-story house. We were just kids and had nothing to do. We saw that there was a broken window that led to the basement, and it looked like someone else was there before us. Being curious kids, we looked inside. It looked abandoned, and we did not see any Do Not Trespass signs, so we went in through the window, then went upstairs. It was empty, all but a few old things lying on the floor. It was daylight, and we just thought this would be a good place to get out of the weather. Back in those days, kids weren't in the house and always had to entertain ourselves. Our parents did not care as long as we stayed out of trouble. Looking around, someone found this old double-barrel shotgun with rabbit-ear hammers. That's about all that drew our interest. The gun was rusty and dirty, but we figured we could oil it and make it work so we could hunt with it because a lot of woods was right behind our home, and we were always in the woods like almost every day. That is all we took.

But not long after or in between times, we used the old place to hang out and bring pop and snacks and there were some other kids who also found and used the place. They too used it as a clubhouse. The place was nasty and smelled like mildew, but we didn't care. The other kids were Loui, Bill Dooley, Terry Green, and a kid they nicknamed Maynard. I did not know their part of this story until recently. But apparently, Terry Green took some tank tops and some German metals he had found in a box. We got bored with the place and did not go there too much, but one day, the other kids went back to hang out as usual. They went in one by one and started up the old stairs They were racing to see who could be first to get up there and eat the chips and stuff. The first kid had long legs and skipped steps going up and so did another, and finally Terry just figured he would walk up. His foot caught a trip wire to a large pipe bomb booby trap. Boom! All the boys were injured from the shrapnel, except for Terry Green. He caught right in the belly!

Somehow he managed to crawl out the window and die in the tall grass. I heard the ambulances and sirens, so I went there and asked what happened and someone said some kid was killed in that house. I was so afraid because I and my friends were hanging out in that place! I left and kept my mouth shut. As time went on, the story unfolded and what had happened was this German man supposedly lived in Illinois, had a brother in the Navy, who was a bomb expert, and had set a pipe bomb under the staircase to kill whoever tripped the wire. This was set for me and my friends as well as these other kids.

When the trial came out, the injured boys were interrogated and made out to look like hoodlums who broke in to this house to rob it. But that was not their our intention. They nor us were not violent kids; we were just kids. We never saw a warning sign and have been in there many times prior. As the trial went on, the defense stated that the jersey shirts that Terry Green had taken to wear were those that belonged to Olympic track star Jesse Owens. They were lying on the floor, and he did not have a clue. Also, during the trial there were two soldiers in full dress with the defense. The judge also would not let in the press and moved the trial to the basement of the courthouse. Bill Dooley and others found this to be strange. All the medical bills were paid by an unknown party as well.

The man who owned the house was found guilty of manslaughter but spent no time in jail. The kids are now men in their sixties and are still afraid to mention anything about it. We too never spoke about it to anyone.

It was in the fall of 1970. I was a junior in high school and was on the football team. It was October, and I was walking home from school. As I got closer to my home, I saw what appeared to be a lot of companies where I lived. There were cars and trucks and people moving around carrying things. The closer I got, I noticed that they were carrying out furniture. When I got there, I asked a man what they were doing.

He said, "I don't know. I am just helping."

So I finally found the right person and said, "Why are you removing all the furniture?"

He said, "I bought it all for one price."

I stood there in shock while watching my dresser with my clothes being loaded in trucks, along with all the rest of the stuff. Some time passed as I stood in shock and noticed my dad's car coming down the street. He pulled up in the driveway and talked to the man then walked up to me and said, "Your stepmom, Kitty, and I are getting divorced, and the house is in foreclosure."

I must have had this look of disbelief, but he went on to say, "I don't know about you, but I am going to get me a hotel room," and then he got in his car and left me standing there with nowhere to go.

I went from having a home to homeless, just that quick.

Okay, so there I was standing in front of what was home and sat down on the steps, trying to grasp the situation. I have trained myself to be a realist and see things for how they were. I was already at the point of life where nothing surprised me. I just went on to the next move. So after feeling a little sorry for myself, I started thinking what to do. It sounds like my dad was heartless, and at the time, I thought so too. But he was raised with my uncle and did not plan on this family thing to happen anyway. I still loved him. All these memories are about my bloodline dad. My adoptive parents will come up later in my life. I only had the clothes on my back, but I did manage to save the walnut bowl that I made in wood shop and still have it to this day. My sister had been recently divorced, and I remember someone saying she lived all the way across town, but I wasn't exactly sure. My brother Mike was playing in a big rock band, backing up a group called Grand Funk and a few others. He was in for a surprise too when he got home.

My sister Michelle was all messed up from our early years and found a job dancing in a gentleman's club. She was beaten up a few times but stayed at it. I was still dating Pam and was not the type of kid who would intrude on her parents; besides, they were very old school, and a boy was not staying there. Actually, I had to sneak around dating her because her parents thought I was a Mexican, and they were prejudiced people. It was not until she was staying overnight at her best friend's house, Debbie Hallmark, that Debbie's mom called Pam's mom for something and her mom said okay to whatever it was as long as that Kenny kid was not there! Mrs. Hallmark knew me well and knew I showed manners over there. So she asked why, and Pam's mom said, "I don't want her with Mexicans!"

Mrs. Hallmark said, "Kenny is not a Mexican. Kenny is a Indian boy whom I trust more than all the boys who come around!" Pam's mom said, "But his last name is Flores." And Debbie's mom said, "It was a surname because, in the old days, Indians could not use their real names." Pam's mom had a different look then, but I never knew this conversation took place until years later. Anyway, that's why I did not want to be a burden to them. So I walked across town and found about where my sister was staying and asked neighbors if they knew of her or something to get a lead. Someone said, "There is a young lady who drives a blue Volkswagen Beetle. Maybe that's her." Well, I sat on her porch for many hours, and yes, it was her. She was working and got off at midnight at a canning factory in Gary, Indiana, called National Can Co. She pulled up and asked what I was doing over there so late! I began telling her the story. She said, "Well, I only have a one-room apartment and nowhere to put you."

But being a good-hearted mother-hen type, she said, "Okay, but you have to sleep on the floor." That was fine, and I slept there until I could get my head together. The good news for me was I was still working part-time at Bob's 66 Gas Station, so I quit sports and went full-time, but that was after school and weekends, so I saved every penny so I could get some wheels. Back then you did not have to have insurance, and that saved me a lot. Besides, my cars weren't expensive, but they were kept clean and had a good radio. Well, a week later, my brother Mike came back off the road with his band called Ten High. As they were coming through the subdivision, he told them to keep the radio down because it was very late. He had on the old platform shoes and a leather vest with long hair.

First thing he saw was the house was black because no lights were on and thought that was unusual. Then he grabbed the doorknob and saw it was locked, so he went to the basement window where his and my room was and started pecking for me to let him in and soon put his hands together to look inside. No bedroom furniture or me! He walked around the house and saw it was empty! He freaked out! Down the street lived his best friend Jimmy Lambert, so he went down there, and Jimmy let him in with him. Well, a couple of days later, Mike found our sister Toni, and she said, "I don't know what to do! My landlord is going to kick me out if he sees all of us living here!" We did not know what to do, but she always was the kind who could make decisions, so she went looking for a duplex apartment in Portage, Indiana. It was about fifteen miles from school, so I would have to drive every day. I had this old Chevy II Nova, but it ran good. I was a junior in school and had no idea what I was going to do for the rest of my life.

One day, I was introduced to a helicopter pilot for the Army National Guard. He told me if I join I could start attending drills and get paid for them and not have to go to basic training until after I graduate from school. He said they pay like eighty dollars for a once-a-month weekend drill and go to a two-week summer camp once a year. I thought about it and figured I seriously need the money, and by the time I have served my commitment, I will be in my twenties and old enough to know what I want to do in life. So I joined. Now I was going to school, working at the gas station, and I am a soldier. In school, I knew I needed to act a little more responsible, so I saw new freshmen boys and told them all if a bully picks on you, come get me and I will protect you.

The next year, the same thing with those boys. I was getting pretty popular and had a reputation of not taking crap from anyone but not looking for trouble either. I tried to date other girls but was shut down. Not being good at being shut down, I quit looking. Besides, I had enough on my plate. Although I kept all my problems to myself, I really struggled in school as far as grades. One day, they were having this thing called senior day, and you could run for a city office and be in charge for that day. I thought,

Hey! I want to run for fire chief. So I had a bunch of not A students help me with signs. Some signs were even spelled wrong. My nickname in school was always Chief, but some signs spelled Vote for CHEF for Fire CHEF. LOL. Believe it or not, I won! So it was a fun day for me.

Well, back at the gas station, the man who owned it was Bob Austin, and his son and I were good friends. We always worked evenings, and different friends from close by would stop in for a bit on their way to something going on Fridays at the school, maybe a dance or sock hop they used to call it. One of our friends name was Tom Burger. Tom was a nice guy and never caused trouble, but for some reason, my friend Bob Jr.'s dad, Bob Sr., did not like Tom. One Friday evening, Tom was walking by the station while we were working and stopped in just for a moment while he was on his way to a dance. Bob Sr. pulled in and said, "Robert, I don't want him over here hanging around," pointing at Tom. So Tom instantly left. We went on and worked until eleven at closing time, and Tom was on his way back home and stopped for just a moment, and my friend Robert said, "Hey, you need to leave. I will get in trouble if my dad sees you here." About that time, Mr. Austin pulled up on his way home from the bar and drunk. He got out of the car, and Tom left and he went off on his son, my friend, and said, "What did I tell you?" Robert said he wasn't here, but all his dad saw was that he was there and assumed he had been there for quite a while.

Now Robert was a senior in high school, and his dad grabbed a handful of spark plug wires and beat him across his legs and back so severely that Robert could not stand up! My whole outlook changed at that moment about my boss, Robert's dad. I thought, *Why, you creep! I thought if this is what having a dad and mom is like, thank God I don't have one!* Of course, Robert never forgave his dad. Later that year, Bob Sr., my boss, hired this young skanky-looking fourteen-year-old girl, and we were a little confused, but it was his business, not ours. She was a dishwater blond and skinny and not much to look at, but his dad was always messing with her and grabbing her ass, but she acted like she didn't mind. I kept to myself and minded my own business. One day, it was my turn to open the station on Sunday, so I drove over his house to get the cash drawer from his wife, and she told me they were not opening up today and I was not needed anymore. *Really?* Just like that, I am fired? For nothing? Later I found out why. Bob Austin ran away with that fourteen-year-old girl and left his family. He was in his forties! His wife just found out she was pregnant, and she too was in her forties! Robert Jr. was so embarrassed, and the FBI was looking for his dad because he took her to Florida. Wow! What a mess. And I am jobless.

Well, since the gas station is now closed, I still had my once-a-month check from the National Guard, and that helped. I am a senior in high school now and kept all of my problems to myself and hid it by being the class clown. I liked seeing kids laugh. I was very good at drafting, wood, and metal shop. As matter of fact, I always had teachers wanting to buy the things I made in woodshop. I was not very good at art class and had a teacher named Mr. Smith. He was a tall guy with thick glasses and big ears but did the best he could although the kids were always messing with him. One day, Mr. Smith had left the classroom for something, and this boy named Kevin Hurshy was running across the tables. I thought it was stupid, so I minded my own business. Well, Mr. Smith came in the class, and the boy had made his way by my table, and I was looking up at him. Mr. Smith thought I was part of the mayhem and told me to get in the hall! I was thinking, what for?

Then he came out there with this big paddle, and I tried to tell him, "I had nothing to do with it, and why are you not bringing out that kid?" He came up with this: "You are older and should have done something to stop it!" I said I was innocent! He told me to bend over and was intending on swatting me for something I had nothing to do with. Well, a backflash came, and I was beaten before for something I didn't do, and I was not going to let it happen again! I was pissed, and I told him, "If you hit me with that paddle, I am going to take it away and beat your *ass* with it because I did nothing wrong!" I meant every word! I would have done it! I was too old for this shit and had been through enough in my life! Well, he knew I meant it and quietly said, "Well then, get your ass back in class." I started to the door and turned around and said, "Wait a minute! Did you just curse me?" His ears turned red and said just get in there, and I said, "No! You just cursed me, and I am taking you to the office." LOL.

Well, I let him go after I saw he was pretty nervous about that. Well, later through the school year, he was talking about taking some of his artwork to Terre Haute to a show because he was from there. And I said, "My mom who left me as a child lives there" and I came to find out his parents lived near her. We started talking more and more and actually became real good friends. We are very good friends even to this day and stay in contact. I was still dating the same girl named Pam, and she took up a lot of my spare time during that year. I pretty much got along with everyone in school although it was a small school. I think we had a graduating class of one hundred or so. It was toward the end of my senior year that I was told that I had a vacation from my boss at the gas station just before it closed down, so I decided to go on a fishing trip to Kentucky Lake in Kentucky.

My best friend Ronnie Robb, my cousin Davy, and I planned to fish and take a tent. So I went on vacation for about five days. We had to read a road map and took my little Chevy Nova. No one cared if I went. After all, I had no parents and I was on my own. I was very mature at my age and was always in charge of my own safety. Well, we all went. It was a long drive, but we made it. I had just a little money and did not know how much it would cost, but we all pitched in and had gas money and did our own cooking. The first thing when we found a marina was to ask if we could rent a rowboat. The man was kind and offered us a motor, but we couldn't afford it. So we had to row. I was the strongest and oldest, so that was going to be my job. The first thing we did was load up the tent lantern and sleeping bags, etc., in the boat. It was only twelve feet, so with us three and the stuff, it was loaded. We saw an island which didn't look too far off and thought we would head that way. It was way farther than we thought, but I kept rowing.

Before we knew it, this giant barge ship was coming our way. The closer it got, the bigger it got. I was huge!

Well, it was getting close, too close, and started blowing its horn because we were in the way, but I couldn't row any faster. It was right beside us before we knew it! As it passed, it had the monstrous waves that it made and looked taller than the rowboat. As I saw them coming, I had to think quick! I turned the bow of the rowboat into the waves and told the other guys to hold on! The waves hit us, and we were inches from capsizing! We lost out tackle box and some supplies. All I can say is God was watching us that day. After we got stabilized, we decided not to take any more chances and hug the shoreline; that way, any other mishaps, we could swim to shore. The water was full of these aggressive snakes that I later found out were poisonous water moccasins.

Well, we found a place to camp and was really tired, but we had enough stuff in a small tackle box that didn't go over. Well, we managed to catch fish and I was the cook. They were great! So we finally had the tent set up and got the Coleman lantern slit and jumped in the bags and went to sleep. The next morning, I woke up first and thought, Who the hell left the door flap open? Well, the door flap was still zipped, and the big gaping hole? Well, that's where the lantern caught the tent on fire and the canvas had just enough retardant to stop burning. That was the second time we escaped death. Things got a little better the next day because a couple good ol' Southern boys pulled up in their motorboat and talked to us; we all got along good. We told them what we had gone through and let them know we lost our food.

One of them offered us some of their BBQ meat, and we ate it and we thanked them. I said, "That was good stuff. What was it?" He said goat. I said, "Goat?" Well, baggers can't be choosy. Actually, it was good stuff. The next day, we decided to go out in our boat, so we went light with just poles and fishing lures. Well, it was hot, and we were just relaxing in the boat, lying on the benches and floating and looking at the clouds. I looked over the side and saw this thing floating by and didn't know what it was for, then in a bit saw another. They were red. I kept hearing this industrial horn going off, thinking when they going to quit sounding that thing and then put it together. They were sounding it off, trying to warn us kids that we were about to go over the dam!

By that time, the current was pulling us faster and faster! I grabbed the oars and began pulling as hard as I could, rowing as fast as I could and trying to make it to shore, when, all of a sudden, I snapped an oar in half! We were using one paddle and dumped the tackle box and all three of us giving it all. We had to make it to shore. We almost died for the third time! Well, we made it to shore, and I was totally spent and was getting my breath. As I was finally getting relaxed and lying there. I looked at the wash stones I was lying on and—*spiders!* Millions of them! I jumped up and shook myself, totally freaked out, and said, "Let's get back to camp and we are leaving this place in the morning!" Well, the next day, we turned in the boat. We left later than we wanted to, so I drove until I was too tired to drive. I pulled in this park area at midnight and went to sleep to wake up to these little black girls laughing and staring at us through the side window. They had the old-school paper curlers made from newspapers in their hair, and they said to my buddies, "You two better get out of here. You're in the wrong part of town. You guys are in the projects." I told them, "We did not want trouble. We just needed a place to sleep, and we are leaving." Well, we made it home.

The next school day came, and I returned to school. I was called to the office at Edison High School, and the principal wanted to see me. I went in his office, and Mr. Georjakus was his name, and a few other people were there too, including the superintendent of schools. He said, "We would like to know where you have been for the last week." I said, "I was on vacation." He then looked around at all the others and said, "Oh, he was on vacation!" Then he said, "And who told you you could go on vacation?" I said my boss. He told me I had worked there for a year and could take one week for vacation. So then he goes on to say, "Would you like to tell us about it?" I said sure.

So I proceeded to talk about all the events, and he said, "Okay, enough of this! We have rules, and you can't just go on vacation when you feel like it!" I said, "I have been going to school for twelve years and have seen other kids go on vacation, and no one says anything about it so, why can't I have a vacation!" He said, "We have rules and I am going to expel you from school until we speak to your parents! That's all!" So I timed this just right because he did not intimidate me at all, but I kept my cool. I said okay, and as I was walking out the office, I turned around and said, "Can you do me just one favor?" He said, "What is it?" And I said when you find them, "Tell them that I am fine and doing okay." He quickly said, "Wait, wait a minute. What are you saying?" I told him and the rest of them, "I have been basically homeless for a year and a half! I paid my way through school by working at a gas station and driving here every day from Portage, Indiana! My dad and stepmom, I have not heard from or seen, so if you find them, good luck!" Then he paused with this puzzled look and said, "Go back to class, and we will let you know if we need you."

So I went back to class and heard nothing from the office. I was stressed out pretty much all my life because I had to learn how to talk my way out of a lot of situations. I had no one to defend me and never did. I was sleeping at my sister's but totally on my own. It's funny how life gives us our own choices to make. I could have been one of many bad people; it was simply up to me, but I had no desire to hurt, steal, or deliberately do someone wrong. Even though I was close to graduating, I had this depression thing going on. I just wanted to quit school. I felt like no one cared about me, and what was the use? When I was about twelve, I was riding in the car with my dad, and out of the blue, he looked over to me and said, "Nobody cares about you! And they don't want your kids!" I really didn't know how to take that, so I just looked at him and then out the window. I have always had this thing with this delayed reaction to shocking news, so I mulled it over for years. I remembered those words and finally figured it out. I think he was saying we are all on our own in this world. It's everyone for yourself. In other words, if you want to make it in life, it's up to you because no one wants to carry you or have your problems. And as for your kids, they don't want the responsibility of raising your kids either. He also told me, "Remember this! If you are man enough to make a kid, you better be man enough to take care of it because I do not want your kids!" Wow! that went to the heart! But he was trying to make me a responsible man.

W ell, I had missed a couple of days of school and was at my sister's apartment, and she noticed I was home during school days. She was always pretty smart and picked up on a lot of things. She said, "What are you doing home?" She worked middle shift, so she was home in the mornings. I was all depressed and said I quit. She told me, "Oh no, you don't!" And she said she had to quit her senior year because she got pregnant and regretted it every day until she went back to night school and earned her diploma. So she was not going to let me quit! After the scolding, she said with a kind heart and soft words, "I'll tell you what, if you graduate, I will throw you the biggest graduation party in the school!" I thought, really? So now I had something to look forward to because she is the only person who never lied to me, and she meant what she said. I decided that I need to walk a straight line and finish out the year. Come graduation time, our girls student counselor named Mrs. Gleason bought my announcements out of her own money. Wow! I couldn't thank her enough and never forgot her. Looking back, she might have been one of those in the meeting when they were going to expel me and knew my situation. Well, graduation day came, and my brother's band got together and played music at the hall my sister rented, and sure enough, I had a great graduation party, just like she said!

Exactly three days after graduation, my butt was on a jet airliner for the first time headed for Fort Dix, New Jersey, for basic training for the Army. If there was any adjustments needed in my character, I was about to get it. I was afraid and alone, so my instincts were at their sharpest point. I paid attention and listened and also watched other people get in trouble, so I knew what not to say or do. The first week went smooth because they called that reception center. That is when you get all your clothing, haircut, and shots, etc. The very next Monday, while everyone was sleeping, all of a sudden, a loud voice woke others and me, saying, "Get your asses up!" Someone said. "F———U!" And then it was on! "What? What did I hear? Who said that? Who said that?"

Then I looked up, and this huge black man with the most perfectly fitted uniform and this drill sergeant that was throwing over all the bunk beds! His name? Senior Drill Sergeant Hatcher! This man was in perfect shape and not one to mess with, and I instantly knew it! He said, "I will show you all one time how to make your bunk, and when I come back, they had better be right!" I paid attention. Then he returned and found a couple not right and threw, the bunks over and gave us one more chance. Mine was perfect! So were the rest of them. So he said, "I will be back and call formation." We were all shocked and scared as hell. Well, he returned and said, "All you *bitches*, outside and give me a formation!" We all went out, and he began explaining to us how to make a proper formation, and we did. I was standing there so stiff! My chest stuck out and shoulders back because that's what I saw in the movies. I always was one of many facial expressions and people could see pretty much what I was thinking. I even held my breath as he was walking down the line, checking us out.

Then he came to me. I did not make eye contact, and he started checking me out and must have seen how serious I was. Then he took this stick in his hand and tapped my stomach and started smiling a little and said, "Loosen up and step forward." Then went on and picked three others. I found out I was going to be a squad leader. Wow! I got to have corporal stripes on my arm and be in charge of ten guys. Now I was never one to abuse power and always was a leader. Also, I knew how to use common sense and follow orders. I knew right away what this man says: do it! Later on, we in my squad were all together, and I told them all, "Look, I did not know I was going to be picked, and it could have been anyone of you picked, and I would have done whatever job you gave me. So you just do your job, and we will all stay out of trouble." We got along great and if there was any problems, I handled it.

Training went good, and we all had our first weekend off. Wow! We stood out like a light bulb! We all had new jeans, new shirts, short haircuts, and the locals all knew it. LOL. We were even allowed to drink! So a couple friends and I, one named Chris Groves, went to the tattoo parlor. We saw a bunch of drunk guys getting tattoos, and they said, "Hey, Kenny, get one like us!" I stood there and stared at all these designs and said to myself, "What do I want to put on my arm that will be there forever?" I could not find one, so they kept pushing me, so I said, "I'll tell you what, let me think about it and we will come back tomorrow." So they quit bugging me.

The very next day, we all woke up with a hangover, and I saw these guys all moaning about how sore their arm was, and I saw the results! It looked painful, and they couldn't touch it for sometime. Needless to say, we never went back to that town. Six months later, we graduated and were soldiers. Being a young guy in the eleventh grade when I signed up, I failed to read the fine print! It stated that in the event that you are needed to be activated, you will comply. Well, some parts of my engineering unit were activated to Vietnam. I thought for sure I would be activated to relieve soldiers over there, but lucky for me, it was beginning to wind down and they were bringing soldiers back. I was on my way back to Indiana from Fort Dix, New Jersey, and landed at O'Hare International Airport in Chicago. I had my uniform on, and it was perfect. I was proud of my accomplishments because I had earned expert in hand grenade, rifle, and automatic rifle. I had my badges on, and a beautiful girl my age was looking at me, and I smiled at her and thought to myself, *Wow! I think she wants to talk to me!* She then started walking toward me, and I was getting excited inside. Then she dumped her coffee on my uniform and said sorry. I said it's okay, thinking she would stay and talk, but she quickly left.

After I thought it over, I was a little hurt because she was not actually looking at me but my uniform, and she was a protester who did a poor job of acting like she was sorry.

Oh well. so I cleaned it the best I could and caught a bus to where my sister was living and tried to get some plans in order, like look for a job.

Well, my girlfriend's mom and dad worked in Gary, Indiana, at Anderson windshield wiper factory, and they knew people who could help me with a job. I got hired! I stood over this solvent tank of boiling chemicals that really stunk! It was called the degreaser. During that time, I got in trouble horseplaying with some of the women in the punch-press area which was right next to where I worked. We used to roll up an old work glove and throw it at one another now and then. Some of those old gals were really accurate!

Well, one day before Christmas break, the women were slipping in the ladies' bathroom, having a celebration drink, and I was waiting for this one lady friend so I could throw the glove at. Well, she finally came out, and as I drew back, she ducked and I hit some old lady in the head, knocking off her glasses. I told her I was sorry, but she told on me and I was suspended. Wow! I was never fired before, and I felt like a loser. So during that time, I went to US Steel and applied for an apprenticeship to become a boilermaker or fabrication engineer. I took the test and did perfect, except that I totally blew the mathematics part, and that was the most important. All the time I was not paying attention in math class had finally caught up with me. I was embarrassed and really felt like a total looser.

The instructor saw my disappointment, and I explained to him I never took trig or geometry in school and did terrible at algebra. He thought for a moment and said, "Well you mastered the mechanical side of the test, but the math is needed for this kind of work. I'll tell you what, I have a night school that I teach for what you need, and if you are willing to go to my classed and pass, I will give you the job." I was uplifted and said yes! So the man's name was Rick Castellanos, and he signed me up. I went and made straight As! Funny how when we put our mind to something how we can do it. Well, I went through the school and became a boilermaker. My girlfriend became pregnant with our first daughter, Kimberly Marie, and we got married. I was always a responsible man and wanted to give my family what was needed. You see, back then social drinking was acceptable, so on weekends, we had get-togethers at my apartment and talked and smoked.

The apartment we had was very small in the attic of an old house, and we were expecting our second child, so I decided to try and find a house for us all. I went through Moore Reality in East Gary, and they helped us find a nice medium-sized home, so I used my VA benefit and bought it. I cost $15,000 at the time and my payment was $150 a month. The address was 3740 Riverside DR, East Gary, Indiana. While we were living there, I met some friends whom I thought were friends, but they turned out not very good people. I will say his first name but leave out the last: Art. Some old high school friends would pop in on Fridays when we would all get together and play guitars, and some of them smoked weed. Eventually, I smoked a little too. Actually I found out that I would rather be around ten people smoking weed than one drunk on whisky. The worst thing a stoned person will do is maybe ask you for a bite of your hot dog. Drunk people want to fight.

Well, this friend named Art was doing stronger stuff, and one night, about two in the morning, he called me up and said, "Kenny! Come get me!"

I said, "What's wrong?"

"Oh please, just come get me. I am in Gary at a party and something's wrong!"

I said, "Tell me where you are, and I will be there!"

He said, "I will call you back."

I waited wide-awake for the call, and it did not come. I was concerned deeply! The next day, he came over and I asked him what happened. He said, "Oh man, I got ahold of this good shit and took too much, that's all," then went on to say, "Here try it." I said, "No way, man!" Then he began pushing it on me and pushing it on me, saying try it! I just took too much, that's all! I asked, "What is it?" He said, "Rocket fuel!" Rocket fuel? No thanks, then he started really getting angry, saying, "Try it, man!" I just took too much, and now I know how much to take. Dummy me. I gave in against knowing better. I was already contemplating on telling my friends not to bring any more drugs over my house because I have two children that I am responsible for, and I need to be a good responsible father. I said just a little. He thought it was funny and gave me too much!

Instantly I felt this rush going to the top of my head, and it made me very sick and dizzy, and I began to freak out! I was panicking and poisoned! I remember this as clear as a mind could be. I made my way in to this room in my house where the window fan was blowing, and with a sincere heart and prayer, I said, "My God, please forgive me! God, if you let me live through this day, I promise you I will never do any drugs again!" I meant every single word! I kept my promise! All that day I lay sick and poisoned and learned my lesson. The next weekend came and people were stopping by to see if I had any pot. They would leach off me because I had a job and could afford a little. One by one, I told them all I quit! Soon I had no friends because I had nothing for them, and I would not allow it in my house. Now that I got my house in order, I decided that I would apply to the local fire department. The name of the fire department was Camp 133 Fire Department. It got its name because the location was a place where the circus would use as a stopover to camp and water the animals near Deep River, which was across the street of where I lived although it was still located in East Gary.

L ater, East Gary would change the name to Lake Station which it remains to this day. I was accepted! It was exciting, and I wanted to know everything there was to know. After about a year, I was selected to be a lieutenant. The men had a lot of confidence in me, and I loved being a fireman. We soon got a brand-new fire truck; it was a Mack! The chief gave it to me. It was beautiful, and I could drive it good! As time went on, the president of our department for the IVFA, or Indiana Volunteer Fire Department Association, retired and they took a vote for a new representative. They picked me! I was to be the youngest man in Indiana to be president of the IVFA. To this day, I think I still remain the youngest man to hold that position. Next, during my time with them, the members decided to select a few of us to be on a scuba diving team for rescue and recovery. I was one of those and went to diving school for my certification, along with Chief John Mirands, Captain John Sullivan, and Charlie Howell.

One day in the summer, I got a call from the chief, and he said, "Hey, a couple of us are going to do some scuba training at the local clay pit." The clay pit was a big lake that the state dug during the construction of a major bridge for the highway. It was very clear water and a great place to train. Well, I told my wife that I was going with them for a while, and she said no. I asked why. She was mad because it was a moment's decision, and they were on their way to pick me up. Well, despite her not wanting me to go, I had already given them my word. They came over in our rescue truck and we all went. We started getting ready and helping each other, except for Charlie. Charlie was always in a hurry had his gear on.

Before we knew it, we were looking for Charlie, but he had already went in. We were really angry because a major no-no is to dive alone! Never dive alone! All dives are supposed to be planned with those you are with! Well, we figured we would discipline him when we all get finished. Captain Sullivan sat with the truck in case we had any calls. Chief Miranda and I went out together with a plan. We were out about a hundred yards or so in deep water. We had all our stuff on, including our buoyancy compensator vest or scuba life vest with a CO_2 cartridge to set it off in an emergency. The chief was using his snorkel on surface above me about ten feet while I was keeping near as we swam. Suddenly, something caught my attention, and I rolled over to see what the splashing was.

At the moment, I didn't know what he was doing, so I ascended to check him out. He was thrashing vigorously, so I got close to see what it was. He had the look of death! I mean, once you have seen this, you will never forget it! I didn't know it at the time, but his body cramped up. He had eaten before we went diving and got the cramps! He grabbed for my mask, and training quickly came into play. We were told if someone is drowning, they will rip off your face mask and you will both drown! So I did as taught. I placed both of my hands on my mask and spun away. Then I saw him go down for the second time! He is drowning! I then yanked hard on his string for his CO_2 to go off and inflate his vest but to no avail! I didn't work! I found out later his kids were playing with it and deployed it. The third time, he finally went down drowned. I then remembered that when someone is cramped and drowning, get the bent leg and straighten it, then swim them to shore, keeping them up as much as possible.

Well, I got within a few yards from shore, and Sullivan jumped in to finish dragging him in. My lungs were on fire because I hyperventilated dry air, getting him back. I crawled to them and we began CPR and used oxygen, and we revived him. I am not a hero. I only did what was needed to be done. I was never afraid while this took place. I was totally focused on doing what had to be done at the time. Later, Charlie showed up after it was all over and asked what happened.

Back in 1976, when I was a lieutenant on the Camo 133 volunteer fire department, there was a really big guy who applied to join and become a firefighter. We were all a little intimidated because he was a biker for the Invaders Bike Gang out of Gary, Indiana, just a few miles from East Gary, where we were stationed. One of the firemen knew him personally and said he was a good guy. He was a really big and heavy guy with an intimidating look about him, but we soon realized he was a nice guy and a dependable fireman. He was the secretary of his club and everyone in the region knew who the Invaders were and not something to mess with. Big Jim Mott could really be a bully to those he did not know. He was a true outlaw.

One night, he went to a local bar in East Gary called the Coconut Grove on Central Avenue and started bullying this man and his wife who were minding their own business. When drinking, Big Jim would just do whatever he wanted, and no one would mess with him because they were afraid of him. The man and wife were dancing a slow dance on the floor, and Big Jim decided he was going to dance with her. He walked over and just moved in. The lady wanted nothing to do with him, and he bullied her husband and grabbed her and forced himself on her. The man was so angry. He went outside and got a ball bat from his car and returned to see Big Jim forcing himself on his wife. The husband swung the bat at the backside hard enough to put him down, thinking he would knock him out, but it was a harder swing than intended. Big Jim went down!

The rest of the people thought he was knocked out, including the owner, Skeets Skarja. They continued drinking and left him on the floor for quite a while. Finally, after an hour, he did not wake up, so the owner called an ambulance. Big Jim was dead. Soon after, his wife asked us for a fireman's funeral for him because he liked being a fireman. The city of East Gary was very concerned because they knew meant bikers from all across the region would be gathering in their city. Well, we could not deny her wishes because it was his right. We had to put on our dress uniforms and take turns standing on each side of the casket. This entire thing totally freaked me out! I did not like funeral homes in the first place, let alone be forced to stand there. I was a ball of nerves!

So at the visitation, there were so many gang member, some from the Hell's Angels, some from the Sin City Disciples, the Gary Outlaws, and many more. Big Jim had promised his mother that he had quit the bike gang, and she believed him. But when she arrived at the funeral home, to her shock was hundreds of choppers! His mom was pregnant and must have been in her forties. She and Jim's wife didn't get along too well. These bikers were smoking weed, taking pills, had bottles of booze, and was in their colors! I was totally freaking out! They literally took over the place! They didn't start fights with each other because a funeral is truce time.

Well, later that night, a biker walked up to the casket and placed an Invader motorcycle calling card in the hand of Jim. Jim's mother saw this and went off! There was yelling and screaming! Then Big Jim's wife came over and the two women started fist fighting and knocked the coffin over! I was in shock! I was in the scariest movie I could imagine! I almost passed out from fear! The funeral director had to get a cot and take the mother to the hospital! Thank God they stopped visitation. The next day was the funeral. We had dressed up the fire truck and draped a flag over the casket and made out way to the burial site. During the end of the ceremony, a biker took and threw an East Gary police badge in the grave and said, "Until the police do something about this, Big Jim will lie on it!" It was a year later that the Coconut Grove was burnt to the ground, and no suspects were found.

Well, we told Charlie what had happened but was too shook up to scold him for going off on his own. Had the chief gone off on his own, I would not have been able to save his life. I never told many people this story because I never considered myself a hero. I only did what needed to be done. My lungs were messed up for a long time afterward because of hyperventilating the dry air from my scuba tanks. While on that fire department, we received a letter from the mayor of East Gary, stating that they were going to annex that part of town and wanted us to give them all our equipment. Some of these firemen have been on our department for many years, and all the equipment was bought by us. So I, being the president, had to represent us even though I was young. I had a very level head and knew right from wrong.

All these old men voted me in to represent them, and they were counting on me and trusted me. I went to a meeting with the mayor, and he explained that they needed all our equipment and we could have a few men of my choice stay there, but the older guys had to go because the battalion chief wanted some of his men in there. He also told me if I do this, he would make me a captain. Well, the offer sounded great, but I had a responsibility, and that was to do the right thing for all involved. So I went back, and we had a meeting, and a lot of angry men voiced their opinions. After weeks of me going back and forth, we finally read the bylaws and our building agreements and got an attorney. I went back to the mayor and told him the men took a vote and was going to liquidate the equipment and put the money received in to a community center because in the property agreement, when the building and property was donated, it was in contract that it must remain a fire department or a community center.

The mayor told me I had the power as the president of the fire department to make my own decision. I thought it over but decided that these men put their trust and faith in me to do the right thing. So I decided not to sell them down the river and turn my back on them. And so it was, the politicians of East Gary were angry at me, but I told them I was going to honor the veterans and their vote. So the fire department of Camp 133 was dissolved, and the building went on to be a community center.

During this time of life, I was still working at US steel mills in Gary, Indiana, as a boilermaker apprentice. There were four of us to a gang who worked together on broken giant ladles used to carry molten iron by the cranes. It was then that I met what they called a helper. The job of the helper was to find steel that we would need and to assist us when working. His name was George Christian. I was in my twenties, and he was in his midsixties. He was a different kind of guy and mostly kept to himself. For some reason, he liked me. I have always had a way of attracting tough kind of guys. He was very thin, with a big scar across his face and had a very deep voice. I knew he was a tough old man by the way he swung a sledgehammer when we were heating steel plate to bend for certain jobs. Also, there was a man named William Bunton. He was the gang leader and a very smart man too. I was young and paid attention to them. William, or "Red," which we called him, was a captain on a B-24 Liberator. He was the pilot. These guys would open up to me because I earned their trust and respect. They became my mentors. Red was flying a mission over Germany when he got hit by a bomb with shrapnel. He said he was able to hold a circle just long enough to bail out. He had a broken arm and shrapnel in his jaw and neck. When he hit the ground, a farm lady ran to him, yelling, "Nine! Nine!" and he thought, *What is she trying to say?*

Soon, the Germans caught him, and the officer took his hands and, with a hand motion, popped his ears. He could not hear for many months. He was a prisoner of war. He told of maggots in the food, but they ate it because they were starving to death and freezing with few blankets. After the war, he was released and had bowel problems for years. He said if he was at a movie theater, and even though he had to use the restroom, he went right away. I looked up to him because he carried himself as a leader.

But George was a totally different guy. Only a few of us knew his back story, and we kept it to ourselves. George was an ex-convict who spent twenty years in the Michigan City penitentiary for robbing insurance companies and banks. He also stole sugar and liquor from Al Capone's trucks. He told me some stories like the time they were set up to rob Capone's truck and got to it before the Tommy gunman was picked up! He laughed about that as he told me. I knew there was something different about him because when he went home from work, after showering, he always wore a pen-striped, three-piece suit with the old gangster-looking hat. He also told me about the time they robbed a bank. He said they didn't get much, maybe five thousand or so, but he said to me during the lineup that they brought in the teller from the bank.

He said, "I know she fingered me, but she kept looking away," and he didn't get charged. He laughed and said the banks are crooked as we were. Then he read the newspaper and saw the headline where the bank was robbed for ten thousand dollars!

He laughed and said, "The lady who fingered me was told not to pick me."

While he was in prison, he got a degree in dentistry and became a dentist for the inmates. He did a lot of wheeling and dealing and was sending money to his sister to put in the bank because he wanted to open a nightclub, first-class dance hall with a glass floor. But the prison found out and confiscated his account. He broke out of prison two times during his twenty-year stay but got caught. He told me he had no kids and wanted to leave his house and ten acres to me, but his two nephews found out. When George was dying of throat cancer, I would go over frequently, but his nephews would come to the door and say he is sleeping, so I said I will come back tomorrow. Then the next day? Same line. All this time, they were telling him that I didn't care about him, and he died angry at me, thinking I never came to see him while he was dying. Needless to say, he did not leave me anything. Funny how people gather around like buzzards waiting for someone to die to get what they can, even though they have never been there for him.

As time passed, I left there and put in an application in for Bethlehem Steel in Chesterton, Indiana. I left US Steel and began working on March 18, 1974. I went on to become a heating and air-conditioning repairman, working my way up from a helper or assistant to a repairman. I eventually took seven different tests. Each section had seven parts, and if you fail one part, you fail that entire section.

Well, I took all forty nine tests during a span of time and became an A rate or multi-craftsman. I really enjoyed working and fixing things and also use my boilermaker training to fabricate giant air conditioner stands for industrial equipment. One day, while driving home from work, I was getting off the expressway and made the Clover Leaf exit on to Ripley Street. The moment I got on top of the viaduct, I caught something out of the corner of my eye. Off the ramp, I saw a woman jump out of a moving car! She skidded down the concrete, so I went off that ramp to help her. All this happened in a split second! So I stopped, and she was all scratched up and bleeding bad! I got her in, and she was screaming! He's going to kill me! I tried to calm her down, but at the same time, I understood her emotions too. I finally earned her trust by using emergency medical training that I learned from the fire department and from military trauma training.

I earned her trust, and she said the best she could. She had been kidnapped and raped! The kidnapper had her car, and all her keys and purse was in there! He told her if she told anyone, he would kill her kids! He was taking her somewhere to kill her, and she knew it! I was in pretty good shape back then and was not afraid of taking on this guy if he came back! She then went on to explain to me she was working at this restaurant and fancy lounge and was getting off work when this guy came at her with a gun and told her to get in her car and give him her keys, then drove her to a place and raped her. I knew of the place where she worked it was called The Spa. It was in Chesterton, Indiana, just off of HWY 20. From where I picked her up, it was about twenty miles away. So I drove her to the police station and went in to help explain all of what I knew, and they handled it from there. I went home and had a few cold beers to collect myself. I never told many people about that story either because, again, I did not feel like a hero and did not want the attention.

While still living there at the same house near Deep River, I used to go bow fishing and shoot carp fish. I got pretty good at it and gave them away to people fishing on the river. One day, on a weekend, I was with my wife, visiting her mom and dad with our two girls, and returned home to the back door, kicked in, and all the drawers tossed on the floor! We were robbed! They stole my hunting guns and our stereo and other things. I was really depressed! Well, the police didn't catch anyone, so time went on, and again, I got robbed, so I asked all the kids on the block to help me and I would give them a reward. It was not long that they told me who it was, and I had him arrested. I got to thinking this is enough! I decided that I need to get out of that city and look for a place in the country. I was talking to some guys at work, and they told me of a guy who has two acres south of Knox. It was a long drive, but a friend whom I worked with lived near the place, and he said if I move there, I could carpool with him. That sounded good, but actually, it was a very stupid idea.

Again, I had no one to help me make serious decisions, and I am only about twenty-four years old with two little girls and a wife. The land was great, but the home? Well, it was a piece of junk double-wide that had been folded up. Back years ago, someone had an idea to take two trailers and slide one in to the other for transportation. Well, this one was supposedly all there but had to be put back together. I paid the guy ten thousand with the profits from my house that I sold and had this dream of making it a home in the country. When I got to really checking out what it was going to take, I began thinking. What was I thinking! So I told myself that I would make it livable and save up to build a house. Well, the modular was sunk in mud and had to be moved, so I used two twenty-ton jacks to try and lift it and blew the seals out of both jacks because of the suction from the buried wheels and axles. With a little help from some friends, we got tires for it fixed, and then I hired a bulldozer with a ball big enough to drag it where I wanted it.

The thing had a hydraulic pump on the tongue and was supposed to be used to jack the two halves apart. Not so! It would not open! Now what! We decided to set small telephone poles about ten feet apart in the ground at an angle and used long hoists to manually jack it open, but only part of it was moving. Finally, after many hours of frustration and not knowing what was keeping it from expanding, we finally crawled under with a cutting torch and burned the cables which were supposed to roll on pulleys. Boom! It jumped apart and finally opened. I have stressed out my family and myself, thinking, what the hell did I do to my family! I worked tirelessly for weeks all by myself, trying to put this thing together with no directions and little tools.

One day, I was mentally so low that I just sat in a corner and had a long talk with God and asked for some help because I don't know what I am doing. Things started coming together after that. My prayer helped me. Well, I finally got it somewhat livable and then had to learn how to hand drive a well for water. My friends came over—Willis Combs, Terry Cable whom we called Red Man because he had red hair and pretty short but stout, Dale, and John. I learned the hard way how to do this and I saw to it that there was a lot of cold beer for the guys. We beat and we beat and beat for hours with this man-made post pounder and kept testing, but no water. Finally, Will's dad came over and said he knows a good water witcher we were up for anything at that point.

Well, this old preacher man with a wrinkled white shirt on and black pants came over, and he went to a tree nearby. As I watched him, I had my doubts, but I trusted he knew what he was doing. He selected a fresh branch in a Y shape and came back. He started walking with that thing, and it started pointing about two feet from where we were pounding our pipe! He said, "Here's your vein!" I said, "Can I try?" And sure enough, that thing went to the same spot, and I was holding it tight! Well, we started pounding there, and before you know it, we had water! Cold water! Now I am a believer! We all quit for the day because we all had arms that felt like noodles.

Well, after getting water, I was relieved that we could shower. I had to start learning country life the hard way and soon! Living in the rural twelve miles from town meant buying extra everything. Many times I questioned my choice and wish I had some kind of guidance to help me with major decisions. Out here, there was no city water and no natural gas, so the next thing I had to do was get a propane tank out here so we could have hot water. I was broke! I had used everything I had to set up this place. I sold whatever I could at a cheap price to get as much as I could in order to pay a deposit for the tank. I called for the tank to be delivered, and now they said I have to purchase a minimum of two hundred gallons of LP for them to deliver! I did not have it, so I called the last person on earth to maybe help me. That person was my birth dad, Mike. He said, "I would like to help you, but I'm broke right now." I was again destroyed! I ended up going to the Bethlehem Steel Credit Union because I heard they would give me a signature loan for up to one thousand dollars with a high interest rate.

Even though I worked in the steel mill, I was at the bottom of the pay at this time of life and would not advance for years to come. Well, I got the loan, and we had gas. I had no yard and no driveway because I could not afford it. It took me an hour and fifteen minutes one way from here to work. The carpool helped me with wear and tear on my used car, but nevertheless, I will be spending about three hours of my life traveling to and from work for the next twenty-five years! During this time, my wife had some depression problems going on, but I did not know anything about depression. So I tried to be supportive as much as possible. Back in those days, the way we were raised was adults have a few drinks on the weekends, so we both drank beer when company came over. I always wanted to be a good father and husband and not put my family through what I went through growing up. I don't care what some say when these scholars say we treat out families the way we were treated. That's not at least in my case. I knew I had choices and I saw to it not to be that way.

The trailer, or modular, was finally set up, and we kept it clean inside. I was finally able to focus on other things still needed. Time passed and my wife was drinking while I was at work, and I did not think it was a big deal since she was across the road with our only neighbor, Madlyn. Her husband, Randy, had been making this homemade wine, and they were drinking it. I was finally getting used to the quiet and privacy of country life and was always, since a boy, an outdoors man, and there was a big patch of woods behind my two acres that I owned. Not knowing about the owner, I thought I would go squirrel hunting one morning. I didn't care if I didn't get one. I just loved the woods. I was in heaven! I had gone out a few times and got a couple squirrels, and we cooked them Southern style with gravy and biscuits. This was great!

One day, on a weekend, I went out and was standing in the open where the electrical tower lines pass through, and this old man climbed over his fence and came at me with his gun pointed at me! He was shaking, and this made me nervous. I was taught by an old gangster George Christian, who had spent twenty years in prison for a bank robbery that went bad, that if a man pointing a gun at you is calm, that means he is in control of himself, but a man with a gun pointing at you who is shaking and nervous will shoot you maybe by accident. I remembered that. So there we stood. He was pointing his rifle at me point-blank! He said in a really nervous voice, "Now you, you, get out of here now. You are a scaring my goats!" Always having manners, I replied, "Did I do something wrong, sir?" keeping a keen eye on his trigger finger from the corner of my eye. He said, "You're on private property!" I said, "Do you own this land?" He said, "No, but I am the caretaker." I kept saying things like I didn't know and told him I just moved in and knew all about it already, so as we spoke I kept slowly moving my muzzle toward his belly, and when I finally got it pointed right where I needed it, I said, "Now if you're going to shoot me, you go ahead, but I guarantee you, before I go down, I will put every bullet I have in you!" The look in my eye meant every word!

Well, he knew I meant what I said, and we both slowly lowered our guns. I walked back home so depressed because I thought I moved all the way out here and can't even squirrel hunt. From that moment on, I told myself that if the landowner ever decides to sell those woods, I will, at all cost, have to buy them or deal with this guy forever. One day, God must have known my situation because a few months later, an old fella stopped by and introduced himself and said his name was Ernie Thompson. He was a nice man, and we hit it right off. He was the man who owned the farm next to me and come to find out he owned the woods too! I went on to tell him what had happened to me when I went hunting, and he said, "Oh, that was old man Huffer. He had no right to do that because I never told him to watch my land. Make me an offer and maybe I will sell the woods." I was nervous because I really wanted them but was not financially secure!

So I said, "I don't know what to do. Would you work with me?" He said, "I'll tell you what, I will go to the lawyer with you and sell it on a land contract, which means you make me payments, and when it is paid for on an agreed amount, I will give you the deed to the woods." We came up with a fair price and a payment I could afford, and it was mine! Yay! I will never have to beg permission to go hunting ever again! Thank you, God. I kept my back against the wall paying for it, but I finally got it paid for. To this day, I deer hunt and squirrel hunt in total peace. I started working on my yard, and after getting stuck in my own driveway, I finally got gravel put down.

One day, I was on my way home from work, and I noticed there was a really serious-looking black sky in the north headed toward where we live, so I thought ahead and stopped at the Kentucky Fried Chicken place so just in case we lost power, the family could eat. Soon as I got home, I told everyone to turn off the TV and such because this looks serious. We sat at the table, and my back was at the wall with the window and this thing hit! There I was with a chicken leg in my hand and the window broke! The kids and my wife ran to the hallway. I had to keep my cool because they were all watching me, and I knew if I showed fear, they would fall apart. The trailer shook, and the walls were breathing in and out! so I opened the doors and windows so the house would not implode! Next, the rain was pouring in the house because what had happened was a tornado had taken part of the roof off!

Now I have a serious problem on my hands because of it being a junk trailer that I did not plan on living in forever. I only had minimum insurance of ten thousand dollars on it. The insurance company came out and decided to work with me. I told them I was willing to go in and pay the extra money if they could send out a roofer to just put a small gable roof with shingles on it. So they sent a contractor who did it, and we felt more safe and had no leaks. A couple of years passed, and one day, I was looking the front-room window and saw a big crack, so I looked closer and noticed the wall was bowing in! Now I started really looking at the other walls, and they were slightly bowing too. So I called the insurance company to let them know what was going on. They sent out a man to assess the problem and come to find out the carpenter who did the job was the brother of the insurance agent handling my first case. What happened was the contractor should have put poles in the ground to support the roof structure.

Instead, they built the roof gable right on top of the double-wide. Now on a trailer, the walls were framed up with 2x2s instead of 2x4 studs. The weight was crushing the house and about to collapse on top of us all! Since the insurance company picked the contractor they were responsible, so they agreed to let me get estimates on the damage. In order to fix it, I drew my own plans to redo it. I sent them in, and they agreed to pay for the damage. I decided we need to dig around the entire perimeter and pour a concrete footer, then build a frame to support the roof. Now I knew at this point we need to install windows because the trailer windows will not work. This was going to be the beginning of the domino effect. One thing was going to lead to another. Well, the place looks like a house on the outside but a trailer on the inside. Not good!

A few years went by, and these seven-foot ceilings were not going to work because my grandson/son was growing up fast and tall. I call him my grandson/son because right out of the hospital when he was born, he was put in my arms and I loved it! I adopted him the Indian way to be my son. A man can father a son, but it takes a real man to be a dad. So I had him with me, and he was getting tall. After really thinking it out, I decided I had to figure out how to raise the entire roof. So I got a few carpenters together, and we removed the entire roof all the way down to the original trailer tin roof! I then removed the entire original tin roof. Wow! That was really hard! It was a mess! Again, I am thinking, what the hell did I get myself into now? So I stuck to the plans and kept working steady after work. Most of everything I have done all my life was mostly done by myself until it came to more than I could handle.

elieve it or not, Kenny Jr. and I were sleeping in our beds, looking at the stars, while I paid for a hotel room for my wife to sleep in until we get this new roof built, and the walls extended up because my plan was to go with a nine-foot ceiling. After a couple of weeks, we were finished, but the inside trailer walls were still standing. Next, I removed the entire trailer walls from the inside of the house and dry walled it all. It now was a house that I never planned on staying in. It is a ranch-style-looking home with a new heating system and ductwork. Part of my dreams of living in the country was to have my own private pond, so I decided in this life if there is something you want, either you make it or hire it out. I did not have the money to just pay people for things I always wanted. It seemed everything in my life that I wanted I would have to either trade for it or buy it broken and fix it or just build it myself. So I decided to buy this old junk crane that was built in the forties and hire a lowboy truck to try and drag it home. This was just in the planning stages in my mind.

One day, my brother, my dad, and family members were having a couple of drinks here at my place. We were sitting at the picnic table, and I said I was going to dig a pond, and my dad said, "Where?"

I pointed and said, "Right over there." In a mocking way, he looked at my brother and said, "Did you hear that? He is going to dig a pond."

He had this smirk on his face. I picked up on it and was really angry! I was thinking, *Is that all the faith you have in me to basically call me a dreaming fool?* So I looked him right in the eye and said, "Watch me!"

He then said, "Just how do you plan on building this pond?" I said, "I am going to buy an old dragline crane!"

He looked at my brother and said, "Oh! You hear that? He's going to buy a crane."

Then he looked back at me and said, "Then what are you going to do?"

I said, "I am going to rebuild it."

Again, he looked at my brother and said, "Oh! He is going to rebuild a crane. Where are you going to find this broken crane?"

I replied, "I already found one in a farm field."

He then laughed at me and said, "I got to see this."

I said, "You watch me!"

And that was the end of that discussion. A couple of weeks later, I went to the old farmer named Glen Beem and asked him about this old crane, and he said it used to run but that was a long time ago, and he sold it to me for one thousand dollars. The old dragline crane was made by a company called Lorain. I then hired a lowboy truck, and we dragged it up there with a heavy-duty winch. We brought it here and dropped it off. It sat for a while until I could figure out how this thing was supposed to work. I read up on it and started figuring out its problems. First of all, I had to rebuild the engine. The engine was made in Wisconsin by a company named Wakashau. They made a lot of these engine during World War II. I welded a frame to the back of it and used a big pry bar to put its frame on small pipes to use as rollers.

My friend Willis came over with his tractor and bucket, and we used a chain to lift it once I rolled it out on the frame I built just for that purpose. I then found parts on the computer, such as rings and main and rod bearings. The gaskets, I had to hand make by tracing the part on paper, then bought gasket material. I also found torque specs for the bolts. I was using my cutting torch to burn off the exhaust-pipe bolts, and they were exploding! I didn't know what to think, so I was trying to be more careful, but they kept exploding! I later found out that the military had these engines designed to have exploding bolts so the enemy could not salvage them if it fell in to their hands. I finally finished rebuilding it, and it ran smooth.

Next problem was the brake bands were shot, so I found a place that would put new shoes on the bands. Next? The tracks were loose and chains to drive the tracks were stretched. I made track spacers and found a better chain. Well, I finally got this thing working; it took me a steady six months, but I was happy. I did not discuss any of my progress with family members because they were not interested anyway. I started digging. I thought it was fun, and I got this thing working pretty good! Before I knew it, I had a big hole in the ground. But there was another problem. Where do I put all this dirt? I need a payloader. Well, here I go again. I looked around for a used broken payloader that I could maybe pick up cheap because it needed work. I found one! It was a Hough 70 with a big bucket. The problem? Well, first of all it had a big diesel engine with a cracked head. Also, the pistons were blowing out oil. If that isn't enough, the steering knuckles were shot and could not be steered. The radiator? Shot. And the main bell crank where the bucket pivots was worn out.

This is going to take some serious work, and I have to do it all myself! I rebuilt the engine and found parts in an old heavy equipment scrapyard. I replaced the head and gaskets, then pulled the pistons and replaced the O-rings. Then I welded new bushings in the steering knuckles so it would steer and sat on a stool with a grinder to round out the bushing holes for the bell crank pivot bar. I also found an aftermarket radiator. I did it! Now I can start digging again! Now keep in mind I did all this by myself, and that is the truth! So I drove one hundred and twenty miles to work every day and then came home and did some digging after work. I took off time for family business too.

My wife was getting worse during this time, so I made sure to be there for her and give her support. Her drinking was getting worse, but I did not know it because she got hooked on wine from drinking at the neighbor's house while I was at work, and she had been hiding it. I really couldn't tell because she seemed to have a high tolerance for it.

I stayed home a lot, and when I was digging the pond, I always let her know I will stop at any time she wants me in the house. It was easy because I was just working in our backyard. It took me three years to complete my pond project because I didn't work on it all the time because family was way more important. However, during this time, I had been getting more aware of her drinking and mental disorders. I finally started getting very concerned. Finally, she agreed to go into rehab for alcoholism. I was so relieved! I went there every evening after work to see her. I thought she was going to be okay. While she was in there, I asked a lot of questions on what I could do to do my part. They gave me suggestions like maybe new furniture or a carpet and things like that. I was never a woman hitter or abuser, so I could not figure out why all this happened.

So while she was in there, I wanted to really make her happy when she came back home, so I bought a new front-room set and bought new carpet too. Also, I rebuilt the back porch completely brand-new. I went to pick her up to bring her home, and she acted strange, but I tried to be in a upbeat mood and tried to make her happy. We came home, and I showed her the things I did to try and make changes. I have always been an excellent cook and made her her favorite meal—Southern fried chicken and all the fixings. When I had set the table and had it all ready to eat, I was looking at her and noticed these big red blotches on her face and neck. Came to find out she had signed a paper for them to give her a prescription for these pills that if you drink on them, you could die and they would not be responsible. I said, "What's wrong?" She looked at me and said, "I took a drink."

I said, "That's impossible!" I went through the entire house and removed it! She then said, "I had a Pizza Hut plastic glass up in the cabinet and wiped the gnats away and drank it." I froze and was in shock! I was stunned! I was in disbelief! I was destroyed! I am a man who never cries, but I had to walk away and stand in our bedroom and cried. I could not believe it. It took a couple of days before I could gather my thoughts, then I decided to call that rehab place and launch a complaint. They said to bring her back. I said, "Good luck with that! She is not going to want to go right back where you had her for thirty days!" I finally called a very good friend of ours named Marilyn. Marilyn talked her in to going back. This time, they brought in a doctor from Michigan to give her a complete mental evaluation. Toward the end, he called me in to his office, and boy, did I have the questions. This was a very smart man who told me things that only I knew about her.

For one, he said, "Your wife has agoraphobia. She has to make sure the curtains are closed and constantly checks that the doors are locked. She also has paranoia, depression, and has subtle frontal lobe damage. This means given a certain amount of tasks, she cannot see the end result. She is also suicidal, so I need to remove firearms from the house." Being an outdoors man all my life, I decided to buy the best gun vault on the market and removed all firearms from the house to the pole barn. Well, I said, "What can I do?" He replied, "You just have to be her cornerstone." Well, it was not long that she went back to the wine and chain-smoking. There was nothing I could do. She would have it everywhere and tell me when she was low to go get her some wine and I would say no, but if I said no, she would go get it herself, and I was afraid she would get in a wreck and someone or she would get injured. So I had to get it to keep her off the road. She tried to commit suicide many times, and I had to have her arrested for her own safety. Although she went back to her drinking, she got to where she was stable and seemed to be enough under control of her intake. I t gave me enough time to finish my pond although the project took three years of family stress.

My daughters stayed away from home as much as possible. I finally sold all my equipment and put grass around the pond. I always wanted to get in to acting throughout my life but could not do it because I always needed to be near home because of family responsibilities and my wife's mental disabilities. I was asked by my nephew who knew the situation. He said, "Uncle Kenny? How do you do it?" Meaning, my wife's situation.

I said to him, "I am your example, Michael. When you marry someone, you never know what might happen to them, but it is my job to try and take care of her the best I can."

Now while my wife, Pam, was struggling with her disabilities, I had my own that were getting worse. While serving in the military, one year we were on a two-week activation maneuver in Grayling, Michigan. I was messing around, playing catch with a football and made some diving catches because that's how we as kids played. You see, we always gave it our all when playing baseball or football in the sandlots that we fixed up for ourselves. I was approached by a couple of fellow soldiers. They had been watching me and said, "Hey! That's some good catching. Can you play baseball?" I said sure!

I had no idea of what they were thinking, then one said, "We have a company baseball team and our outfielder is sick. Would you like to try out?"

I was thinking, *Try out? What does that mean? I never tried out to play a game before.* Then they went on to explain. "You see, the Army takes their baseball team really seriously and not just anyone is asked, but we would like to see how you do in a game coming up. Are you interested?"

I said, "Sure, it sounds like fun."

So soon after, there I was in center field; the game was close! I never was one to get nervous in a close game. I would just do my part if it came to me. Sure enough, it was the last inning, and the other team was up to bat with a runner on third base and one on second base with two outs. These guys were really good. They were better than anyone I have ever played with in my life! Well, the batter was up, and I bent slightly, watching intensely! He hit a line drive between center and left field but closer to me, so I ran as fast as I could! I could see I was going to be a little short, so I stretched out and dove in a horizontal shape, catching and holding the ball! Actually, I knew it was a good catch but didn't know just how important it was. We won! And I was the hero and didn't even know it. Each company has a team and they play off for the battalion trophy. The company commanders all took this bragging thing very seriously and took really good care of their baseball players. I was in something bigger than I have ever been in before, and I was starting to understand it. We all even got out of work in order to practice for this big event! We were one of the two finalists and about to play the battalion championship. They even had the jeeps made up for the parade.

Well, game time came and I was as ready as I could be. The game was zero to zero at the bottom of the ninth inning, and the other team was just getting up to bat. The sick fellow returned so they kept me in and put me in right field. The batter hit one deep, and it hung up real high coming to me. I turned and ran toward the fence full speed, looking up, and thought to myself, *This is mine!* But when I planted my spike to make a sudden stop, being sideways to the ball, there was a small hole right where I stepped! Snap! I snapped my leg right at the knee! Down I went. I stood up to run to the ball and fell! My right knee was broken! I kept yelling for them to call time, but the next batter saw I was struggling and hit it right to me on the ground! Down I went, and we lost the game.

I went to the hospital and was told by the doctor that he never saw so much damage in a knee before. I returned home to see a surgeon and was out of work at my normal job and had to apply for sick pay. The problem was, the steel mill where I working at the time was arguing with the department of defense on who should be paying while laid up. I had no income! We had no money for food, so I went to the human services, and they treated me like I never worked in my life! I was an emotional crippled wreck. Finally, I got some food stamps, and we made it until they got it straightened out with my pay. I had the knee surgery, but it never stopped hurting, so I learned how to live with the pain. Then I was having breathing disorders. I could not figure it out. I would sometimes cough up blood, but the doctor said it was just a lung infection.

One day, I was trying to help some old people that I knew by trying to fix their air conditioner, and it was on their roof, but they had a wall made of railroad ties that I could jump to the ground from. I was getting off the roof and got to the railroad tie fence and decided to jump by using my good leg to help me land, but I lost my balance and hit the ground in an awkward way, causing a snap in my back. Great! Bad knee, messed-up back, and breathing problems. Well, time went on and my bad leg was getting crooked more and more by the year. My dad was volunteering for the VA and told them about my knee problems, so they made me an appointment and saw that it was not repairable. I will need a prosthesis or a knee replacement.

The knee replacement was done, and they awarded me a disability percentage. Later in life, I found out that I have asbestosis. That really scared me because I know the outcome of that. I had contacted it from the military because the insulation for the power boats we had was wrapped in it with expanded metal, and every year my job was to use a wire wheel to clean the exhaust system with no protection.

So the military also awarded me an increase for that, which really helped financially. I am a DAV. I have many problems but hide them from people. I take pain pills to survive and get things done that need to be done around here. But it is catching up with me. I am not one who wants people to feel sorry for me. This is why I don't tell people my problems.

As the years passed, my wife began getting worse. I tried to tell her family, but no one seemed interested, so I held it all in and dealt with it the best I could. Oh yes, there were times I wanted to get a divorce because she was getting more and more violent when she had too much. She got a small job at the local farm store and had an episode at work, so they took her to the hospital and called me at work. I went right there and they had released her. I thought that was strange! I asked her what happened, and she said, "I am okay. I just got sick."

Well, that answer wasn't good enough, so I asked the hospital, and they told me they gave her a pain shot and released her. The next day, I called our family doctor, Dr. Dalphond, and he said he can't discuss it with me, and I told him, "I am her husband! You better let me know!" He said, "Since you put it that way, your wife has cirrhosis of the liver, and if she does not stop drinking, she won't last long." I went home and she was drunk. I begged her to try and stop because of what I found out. She didn't say anything. The reason she was getting so violent and out of her mind was because the alcohol was going straight to her blood with no filter. The doctor told me to leave her, and I said, "How can I or anyone with a conscience leave a person with an addiction and a mental handicap?" Needless to say, he was no longer our family doctor.

So after we got rid of the doctor who never seemed to address her problems and my questions, I continued working in the steel mills and really tried to hold in my personal problems. I had a partner who literally carried me because he had also been my best friend. His name is Darryl Fasel; he was a very honest man with values and a hard worker. He did not gossip and understood the situation, but she hid her problems so good that even he questioned some of my stories, but only in his mind, until one day, we had a small party here because the other family members wanted to have a get-together and set up the family band and play music and socialize. It was then when Darryl saw the real side of her when she came out of the house. She normally did not socialize with people because she would rather stay in so no one would see the real side. She came outside, and Darryl went to talk to her, and she was literally out of her mind and did not recognize him, and he told me he watched her for a while and realized all this time I was saying the truth.

He then told me his previous thoughts and gave me a serious apology. But I said, "It's all right. You or no one really knew." She also thought my sister was a lady; she did not know and accused her of being my girlfriend. As the problem got worse, one day, she threw a butcher knife at me and just missed my liver, and it stuck in the wall! I was getting to the point where I wish she would pass out because I never knew what was next, and I knew if she was sleeping, I would be okay. But I was hopeful she might stop, but that was not going to happen.

One evening, she was out of it and insisted that I take her to get an ice-cream cone, but in this small town, we had no Dairy Queen, but we had a McDonald's, and I knew they had one. I pulled up to the order screen, and she started screaming at me while the lady was listening and said, "I *said* I want Dairy Queen!" I was embarrassed and canceled the order. At this point, there was no reasoning, and my stomach was turning and burning. So I thought maybe if I could get her to eat something she might calm down. So I convinced her to let me take her to Taco Bell. I pulled up to the window to place an order, but she started yelling, "I don't like their tacos!" I was so upset that I was going blank and getting a pain in my chest. It was a blur, and I asked the lady for some kind of tacos just so I could get out of line. I didn't even know what I ordered.

As I was trying my best to talk to the lady at the order screen, Pam started beating on the dashboard and screaming, "He's beating me up! Ouch! Help!" I should have had a stroke but somehow pulled forward to get the order, and the lady at the window and the other employees were looking at me like, "You no good!" I was so embarrassed! As we pulled off, she started laughing at me like it was a funny joke. Wow! What a nightmare. I was not myself at work, and it was starting to show. I could not handle it anymore. I was about to snap mentally but seemed to hold on. I went to church and read the Bible one line at a time so I could really understand it and perhaps find some inner strength. My closest friends included Jim Moore. He was a loving friend with compassion and tried his best to give me support. Actually, the only peace I had was the ride to and from work—that is, until I got close to home. As far as dreams of trying to get into acting, I knew I could not do that because I needed to be near home always. One day, a friend of mine who never spoke much set a card on the lunch table where I sat at work, and he said, "I found this. It may mean nothing, but I thought of you. Do whatever you want with it."

I looked at it and saw it was a place for counselling. A few days went by and I knew I needed help, so I went to the VA and asked for a counselor. They set me up with one, and I started telling everything that I was going through. He really helped me and put me on a medication to help me be calm. Again, she had lost her mind and called the doctor and told him she was going to kill herself. He said to her to put me on the phone. He went on to tell me if I did not take her to the hospital, I could be accountable if she did it! I was scared as hell! So I tried to take her to the ER and called an ambulance. When the ambulance showed up, she would not go. I had no choice but call the sheriff's department to have her transported. They kept her for hours, and she almost convinced them she was okay until she got angry and said, "Maybe I will just kill myself! Bingo!"

Now the ball is in their hands, and they decided to put her in ICU under suicide watch. When she got in there, she told the nurse, "I am going home." And this big nurse said, "No, honey, you are our responsibility, and I have ways to make you stay! We can do this the easy way or the hard way." And I saw this big needle behind her back.

Needless to say, she stayed there. The next day, a kind lady asked me if I could talk to her and I said yes. She said she was going to be Pam's case worker. She went on to ask me the same questions that the rehab centers asked, such as, are you mean to her? I said no. Do you mentally abuse her? And so on. I told her and all of them that I do all the cooking, clean the house, wash the dishes, do the shopping and outside chores, along with going to work. They wanted her in rehab, and I said good. Every time she went in there, I had a small spark of hope and would get some relief too. I decided to take on a hobby building RC airplanes to keep my mind busy in a spare room in our house, thinking that if she needed me, I would be right there and could stop what I was doing instantly. I really felt sorry for her because I knew she was really messed up, and I could not ever leave her in this condition. I was and to this day a dependable, nonviolent person.

Well, my own disabilities were working on me, and I had to retire from the steel mills. This was in a way better because I would be home all the time. Well, Pam had another episode and was put back in to rehab, but they would only allowed her to stay for two weeks because we had maxed out our insurance for this. They set her up with a psychiatrist who put her on psychic drugs for all her mental problems, but she lied and said she was not drinking anymore. Now she is not only a wino addicted to one gallon a day with serious liver problems, she is also known for drugs and alcohol! I tried to explain to the doctor, but she pretty much let me know she was the doctor, not me. Well, after retiring from the mills, I needed extra money.

So I applied to the Stark County Sheriff's Department. I was a jailer and a reserve deputy. I had a police pistol it was a Glock 40 automatic. I always knew to not let her have access to it in working order, so I kept the bullets and magazine locked up in my gun vault at all times. After working there for a year, I knew I could leave the frame in its holster. I made a habit of removing the magazine and pulling it back to always check the inside of the barrel before hanging my duty belt in the closet. This worked out okay, and it was habit for a couple of years. I enjoyed working with the officers and going on the road alone in a squad car.

With these pills Pam was on seemed to make her sleep more, but she still kept drinking. One day, my daughter Stayce came home from North Carolina and went shopping at Walmart. She wanted to surprise me with something, but I said, "Thank you, dear, but I don't need anything." She insisted and asked what type of bullets does my officers pistol take. She said, "I can practice with some," so I told her. I was working outside when she and my granddaughters came back. When I came in, I saw the box on the table and instantly took the box outside to the vault and locked them up. A few months passed and Pam asked me to take her to a rehab because she was in too much pain and wanted to try and quit drinking. I said yes, and I called my oldest daughter and she came over.

We called around different facilities, and my daughter wanted to take her because she was an LPN and could explain the situation better than me. We all agreed. Well, about one in the morning, they both came back home, and I woke up and asked, "Why are you both back?" They said,

"It's all about the money, and they misdiagnosed her." My daughter was angry. My daughter Kim was staying here at the time with my other two grandsons Randy and John because her husband was in jail for drugs. I didn't mind because she was helping around the house. About a week later, I decided to go to the jail and talk to the guys. I asked Pam if she was going to be okay while I was gone, and I would not be gone long. I was really relieved because she had not taken a drink for about three days! She was quiet and calm, so I gave her a kiss and said I love you with a smile and she said I love you too. I got in my truck and started it up and was sitting there looking at the gauges and letting it warm a little and heard a boom! Then a yell. I didn't think much about it because my neighbor across the road shot his pistol now and then, and I thought he startled his wife and it was her who yelled at him.

The next thing that happened was my ten-year-old grandson John ran out to the truck and said, "Papa! Nanna just shot herself!" I remember thinking, *No way! There are no bullets in that pistol.* I ran in, and sure enough, she shot herself in the heart. What happened was a couple of months before when my daughter bought that box of bullets, she apparently snuck out one and had it hidden. I was in shock and would not accept this. My worst fear in life came to a reality. I was always afraid of my wife dying before me. As I write this, my eyes are glossy with this memory. If you love someone, it is the absolute worst thing to witness. She left a suicide note that she must have written sometime earlier, but I could not bring myself to read it although the sheriff told me there was one. I had to step down from working as a deputy because I could not focus on anything. Kenny Jr. was a star football player who was contacted by many division one teams, but he lost his direction and started going wild because I could not be there for him and got into trouble for breaking and entering a few places. He was caught and went to a detention center for boys. Our lives were both messed up over this tragic incident.

Now the things that happened to my wife and me were a hard thing to go through although it was not always that way. Pam was a very kind and quiet person inside and was not mean when she did not drink. We were married for thirty-five years, and all the mental illness and alcoholism did not get bad until the last twelve years of our marriage. I found out from a very good psychiatrist that she had frontal lobe damage, along with depression. After telling her parents about this, her mother told me that when she was a little girl, she fell and hit her forehead really hard on the edge of the concrete steps at their house. She was never the same. I wondered, why didn't you ever tell me this? Pam's dad was very mean to her, and she was always afraid of her parents. She needed me because I was a decision maker and understood her. She always had emotional problems and cried for no reason sometimes. I was her cornerstone and her protector. The doctor also told me since she had the other mental problems, she drank to fight the depression but got hooked.

The early years in our marriage, she would cry sometimes after having sex. I was totally confused and felt bad, thinking maybe I should not do that. One day, she told me a story about this man whom her dad hired to do the air-conditioning repair work had violated her when she was a little girl. His name was Bob Fuller. He had a business in East Gary, Indiana. He sold boats and did air-conditioning work. One day, he was in the basement looking at the furnace, and out of curiosity, she went down there and he took advantage of her. She said that she told her mom, and her mom scolded her and said, "That's what you get for going down there!" I thought, really? You blamed your child for what this creep did to her? And you did not call the police? Her parents were strange and did not want attention. Back in the early 60s when this terrible thing happened to Pam. She held this in all her life. I never really got along with her dad. We were totally opposite although I did not argue with him because my wife would get upset. I did find out that the mother of Pam's dad was supposedly raped, and he was born and kept in an orphanage home his younger life so other family members would not know. Pam was a pretty girl and was treated differently than her two sisters. I believe all her past that she held in had been why she got worse as she got older.

ll I know is that I was a good husband or the best I could be to her. I had a hard time getting over losing her because I have never been with any other woman; all I had ever known was her. Now back to my young life with my birth dad. Although he never showed his feelings, he did try to give me support the best he could. My dad seemed like a cold person, but he felt bad too and gave me support. Thinking back about my dad, Mike, he was a giving man who was not raised up in a normal family and lived on the streets where he, too, had to figure out how to make it in life. I can't blame him for how I was raised because he didn't know what to do with four kids when he took us from our birth mother. I remember him coming home when we were all together at the house on Vigo Street drunk and going to bed singing Indian songs and chants to put himself to sleep. He saw to it my brother and I were taught the Indian way. He was given the name that was on a birth certificate Margaret Flores. He had to get that changed, like I said earlier in this book.

My grandmother had a couple girls from another man who died as babies and sent my dad to school with one of those certificates with a girl's name because Grandmother could not read. My dad struggled all his life and was raised by Chief Lone Eagle, my uncle. Chief Lone Eagle was a world heavyweight wrestling champion from 1948 to 1952. He taught my dad all about our heritage as an Osage Indian. He also was an advocate for Native American rights and education. My dad was told that his dad died in the back alleys of Chicago as an alcoholic. Dad always spoke of changing his name and going back to the last name of Eagle but didn't get around to it. My dad had his ways but was not a hateful man; he just was not a good daddy because he didn't know how to be. So he made me grow up tough because he knew I would not make it if I was not streetwise and mentally tough.

It was back in 1989 that my uncle died at the age of eighty-four years old. I was thirty-nine years old. My dad always tried to go out to the bar with my brother Mike and me to keep close. One day, not long after my uncle passed away, my dad wanted to meet up with my brother Mike and me at a lounge in Bass Lake, Indiana. We were having a great time, and then dad started hitting his beer glass with a spoon to get everyone's attention. The place was packed on a Saturday, and he said, "I would like to make an announcement! Our chief had recently passed away, and out of all the boys in the family, he chose one of my two boys and asked me to give his name to one." I was thinking, *Wow! My brother Mike is going to get his name!* Then he went on to say, "This boy was chosen before his death by him, and he wants my son Kenny to be our honorary chief!"

Wow! I was scared! I thought to myself, *What do I do with this kind of honor?* I did not feel like I deserve this, but then my dad went on and said, "All drinks are on me for as long as we are here for this naming ceremony. Kenny's name from here on out is Kenny Lone Eagle!" Then he turned to me and said, "Go to court and get your name changed, son." It took some time for me to let this sink in. I asked my dad, "What do I do?"

He said, "You will know what to do as you get older, son." I am now Kenny Lone Eagle. I no longer need to walk around with a surname of Flores. I now have an identity. And so it was I got my name changed in court.

When I was a little boy, my brother and I asked our elders, "Why did we not get registered with our Osage tribe?" And we were scolded by them, saying, "Do not ask that again." And we asked why. We were told, "If we do that, the government will know right where you are!" It was only two generations ago that my great-grandmother and her family went through that. Nowadays, people ask if we have a card like it's some kind of club. The only problems I have ran in to were what I call the Caucasian Indians who found a bloodline link so they could get a card. I have not applied for a card because I figured I would not need any benefits being I was a working man, not needing to rely on living on a reservation. My grandmother received a letter back in the fifties from the Osage reservation but was afraid and threw it in a trunk. My birth mother saw this and really wanted to read it but wasn't able. She seemed to think it had something to do with the oil they found on the reservation.

I went on with the name Kenny Lone Eagle and got adjusted to it with no problem because I now had an identity. I went to work every day and continued raising my son/grandson Kenny Eagle. He went on to play football for Arkansas State at Pine Bluff with now all-star left offensive tackle Terron Armstead for the New Orleans Saints. Kenny played right next to him as left starting guard. He also had offers by some pro teams but decided he had enough. They did, however, win the national championship that year. After my wife passed away, my daughter Stayce introduced me to one of her friends that she worked with down in Ashville, North Carolina. Her name is Linda. Linda, too, was a widow who lost her husband of thirty-five years due to illness. Linda was guardian over her granddaughter named Emily. Emily had this illness called microcephaly and cerebral palsy; she was totally dependent and about sixteen years of age when we met.

Linda and I phone dated for a year really getting to know each other before we started seeing each other. I kept my personal business private, but family members thought I just met her and was going to get married too quickly. Some even went as far as to undermine the relationship with their terrible gossip full of lies and painted Linda as a bad person. They were totally wrong.

It was around that time of my life that I went to a rendezvous in Rochester. There sat an old Indian man signing autographs at a little wooden table. His name was Basil F. Heath. He was an actor who did appearances in movies such as *Bonanza*, *Wagon Train*, *The Virginian*, and many more, but I did not know it at the time.

I walked over and said hi, and he nodded and our eyes locked. We both just stood there with our eyes locked, and he said, pointing his finger at me, "Who are you? You look very familiar, but I can't put my finger on it."

I said, "Do you mind if I sit here with you for a while?"

Excitedly he said, "Yes! Yes, please sit!" He then asked my name and I said it is Lone Eagle. His eyes moved back and forth, searching his memory, then asked, "Where are you from?"

I told him I was from the Gary, Hammond, and Chicago area, and my brother and I used to go with my late uncle Chief Lone Eagle. We used to do appearances with him and did dancing at places like the Enchanted Forest in Chesterton, Indiana. His eyes lit up and said, "I knew it! I knew I saw you somewhere in the past! I knew you as a child, and I was there with you although you were too young to remember!" He had pictures of my uncle and him with Tex Ritter who was a country music star too. We were instantly connected like son and dad.

I told him, "Had I known you were here, I would have brought my headdress."

He said, "My wife is in that building behind us, and she has mine with her. Please go get it and put it on!" I thought, *Wow, what an honor!*

Well, it was like magic the moment I put it on people started gathering around us and asking for pictures with their children and grandparents. We had a fun time. Not long after, I went to visit him and his wife at their home in Rochester, Indiana. They had a small place along the Tippecanoe River. We visited, and I felt like I was family His wife, Roberta, who went by the name Bobbie Bear was the sweetest lady, and we too hit it off great. She used to joke around saying, "Are you sure you're not his kid? You act just like him." Basil and I thought alike. Time went on and I gained his full trust and confidence to where he would tell me things that would only stay in the family, so I gave him my word. Among the Indian people, our word is valuable.

He went on to teach me other traditions of the way of our ancestors that I did not know, for example, if I have a watch on my wrist and you are overwhelmed by its beauty and can't stop looking at it, I am obligated to give it to you because you like it more than I do. So he taught me to never stare at someone's personal things. We got really close, and he and Bobbie really liked Linda and me. We visited often. Basil was up in age, and one day, out of the blue he said he would like to adopt me the Indian way. The

Indian way is good because it is our word, and our word is good. Bobbie was excited to hear this because I would be her son. My birth parents have both passed away at this time, so I figured we can do this and what harm would it do. So we had a small ceremony and told all the people at the Rochester Museum we were going to do this. This way, the items he had placed in the museum would someday be turned over to me. The adoption was not registered in court because we saw no need it was traditionally done, and we were fine with that.

A few years had passed and Basil, also known as Chief White Eagle, was getting ill more often than usual due to his age. I had to take him to doctors' appointments more often. I always called him Pops after the adoption. As time went on, Bobbie, whom I called Mom, was having problems coming on too. Linda and I both were taking turns along with the close family friend Shirley and Bill going to doctors' appointments. As time marched on, in some cases, I needed to sign in as a family representative to get them admitted to the ER. We soon found out that our Indian adoption was not good enough to do this in a legal manner. We had medical problems and legal paperwork that needed to be dealt with, and Pops was not able to handle it. We had to make a legal change in order for me to take care of them. They decided to get an attorney and get the adoption legal through the court system.

We discussed it, and I gave my word to take care of them no matter what. So it was done. We went to court in Rochester, Indiana, and the legal adoption was done. I knew my birth father, Mike, well, and he would have agreed with the decision. My name is Kenny Heath although we all agreed to keep my name as Kenny Lone Eagle. Pops had passed during the time the time of the filing and the actual court date, but his name is on my birth certificate. Some family members did not know the story behind this, so they decided to draw their own conclusions. Some thought I lost my mind, but I only did it in order to keep my word and commitment to taking care of them. Bobbie was the best mother anyone could have; she was always giving me things, and I loved her too.

I moved Mom to Winamac, Indiana, closer to me so I could be there to help her as she got more ill. I kept my word. Linda and I took very good care of her, and I bought her a nice little home. She finally passed from cancer, and it was a long terrible battle for her. I went to the nursing home every day to see her until the end. Before she died, I was contacted by a talent scout to see if I had ever acted before and would I be interested in auditioning for a Western movie series. They wanted to see if Steven Seagal would take the part, but he was too busy, so they asked me to do an audition reel and send it to them. Wow, I was excited; my dream of being in an Indian film might happen! Mom was so excited that she started making me clothes and special beadwork. She was a master beadwork person. She made clothes for Pops too and also made his beadwork. She said, "Basil would be so excited if he were here." Well, I did the reel, and they said I knocked it out off the park. I was cast in a movie called *Big Sky*!

It was during that time that I heard on the local radio station that the governor of Indiana was going to be near where I lived in a town called Winamac. He was going to be talking about helping small businesses. At that time, I had an idea how to make a rifle cartridge that would be legal to use here in Indiana to hunt deer instead of shotgun slugs. He would be there that day, so I went to the place kind of early and sat at a table, waiting for him. He arrived and the people said we had to leave because it was for local business people only. A man and his wife argued, saying, "I come here every day at the same time, and I am not leaving," so they said, "Okay, he could stay." He asked me if I would like to sit with him and his wife, and I said yes. Soon all the people started coming in, and then Governor Mike Pence arrived. I sat and listened to him.

Right away, I said to myself, *I like this man!* He had a honest look about him and a character that was calm and intelligent looking. After he was finished talking, I walked up to him, and we began talking about my idea. He asked me if I was Native American, and I said yes. I then told him a little about my ancestral background. He seemed very interested and wanted to continue talking, but his schedule was busy. He told me he was wanting to bring back a Native American commission and asked me if I might be interested in applying. I said I would like to hear more about it. He then took a picture with me, and we connected right away. Then he told his aide to get my information. I went home, and a month or so went by and I received a letter from his office, asking if I would like to apply for a place on the Indiana Native American Indian Affairs Commission, or INAIAC. I filled out the paperwork and sent it in.

Weeks later, I was contacted by his office for an interview. I was among many applicants. I did well on my interview and was chosen. I was so excited that I could represent the Indiana Native Americans. The foundation was to interact with our communities, educate, and bring an awareness. So I did just that. I was always honest and went to schools to teach the children and talked with the Knox superintendent of schools, Mr. Gappa. I talked to the *Northwest Indiana Times* about Native American education in our schools They published the story, and at that same time, Senator Gregg Taylor was pushing a Senate Bill 336, trying to get ethnic education in our schools as part of the curriculum in high schools as an elective to be offered. I was contacted by his office and spoke to a Mr. Gary Holland. Mr. Holland asked me if I would represent the Native Americans toward this bill and speak to the Senate subcommittee in a hearing to be scheduled. I said I would.

So it was passed and signed into law by Governor Eric Holcomb. Governor Pence was asked to be vice president by Mr. Trump, so Eric was nominated as governor. I was given a special award by the National Association for the Advancement of Colored People (NAACP) for my part in this historic bill. I was very honored to receive this award. As far as my commission was going, the board had decided to allocate subcommittees. I was assigned to the health committee; others were assigned to education and other committees. A couple of us were assigned to the civil rights committee. I had no idea at the time, but our chairman of the board was a Potawatomy leader in South Bend, Indiana, and also the chairman of the board with the Four

Winds Casino and also voted as a leader for his people. During this time, Mr. Obama was voted in as president, and it seemed that anyone with a cause decided to push their cause and the news was right with them.

The *Washington Post* came out with this post regarding the National Football League (NFL) and the logo for the Washington Red Skins and how it was racist. That stirred a lot of unrest across the country, and our chairman jumped in on the cause. He seemed to think that the name was coined during the Indian wars, meaning that when bounty hunters rode in to town with saddlebags on their horses, they would be soaked red with scalps; therefore, they got the name Red Skins. He was appalled by this. But the true meaning was the Cherokee warriors took red okra and dried it out to make a paint and would paint their bodies red to intimidate the enemy; therefore, they were called the Red Skins. Either way, he and a couple others, including our director, their goal was to confront Indiana schools with the mascot named Red Skins or anything that they felt was racist. Without the commission knowing, they took it upon themselves to go to a school in Goshen, Indiana. They went to the school board meeting and presented their case. The board, knowing nothing about native education, felt like racists, and that same evening, without going to the community for a vote or tabling the idea in order to research it, they voted to remove the Red Skin name for the school. The community was in shock! There were people crying and totally upset over this.

I felt bad for the community, so I reached out and called the president of the school board and asked her to think it over, but she said they had already voted, and it was over. The next meeting we had in Indianapolis, our director said we had a major victory. Goshen Schools removed the mascot name, and we had a lot to do with this. I interrupted her and said, "We, as a commission, did not have anything to do with this! I joined this commission to interact, educate, and bring awareness to my community and not destroy them! This should have been handled through legislation. It is not our job to destroy communities!"

The next school on the list was in my community, the Knox Red Skins. I said I have a problem because I live there and have never seen racism with our schools and could not punish a community for something they have no idea why they are being punished. The chairman, John Warren, and I exchanged words on how he could not even say the R word. Knowing the next thing to happen would be the same tactic used on Goshen Schools, I set up an appointment with our superintendent, Mr. Gappa, to let him know what was about to unfold. I told him if the local news contacted him to let them know you have a state commissioner for the Indian commission representing the Knox community and to call me and I will be his spokesman. He was so relived because he had no idea how to handle this.

Earlier in the book, I mentioned Chief White Eagle. He lived in a small cottage in Rochester, Indiana. One day, we were sitting around, and I saw this old Winchester rifle in the corner. I knew it was very old because of the patina on the barrel; also, it was octagonal. I said, "Pops? Where did you get that old rifle?" He sat there and said, "When I was at my prime in the movie business, I always made way to visit my Indian fans. One day, I was told by my agent that an old man wanted to see me and asked if I would visit him because he was too ill to see me in person. So I went there with my entourage. We drove to the White Mountains to visit an Apache man. We drove up the mountain through many switchbacks and we drove and drove. Finally we reached the place. I remember it vividly. It was a little one-room cabin. I asked my people to wait outside because it is rude to be asked as a guest and bring in others. It was old Indian tradition." He said with his eyes closed sitting in the recliner, "I went in and there in a bed lay an old man, very sick and dying. He said he was the son or grandson of Geronimo." So White Eagle said, "That's nice to know, my friend." As they were talking, he then told me he noticed the rifle in his corner and politely said, "That's a nice piece." The old man then said, "That is why I wanted you to come up here. It belonged to my dad or his grandfather."

While writing this, I can't remember which one. Anyway, the old man went on to say, "I want to keep this with the Indian people and would like you to have it." Chief White Eagle said, "Thank you, my friend. I will use it in my movies and keep it and not part with it." He then told me they visited for quite sometime before he had to leave. He also kept his word and actually used it in many movies. The rifle has a distinct crack on the right side of the forestock and is recognizable in the pictures taken in Hollywood. I have these pictures in 8×10s. Then Pops opened his eyes and said, "I will leave this and all my clothing to you someday." He passed away in Hickory Creek Nursing Home in Rochester, Indiana, at the age of ninety-four. I think he was in his late thirties when he got the rifle. I now have it.

I had never lost my faith in God, and he has been with me all through my life. I believe I would have never been able to handle the things I have been through without his help. What I mean is, although some of my stories may sound really bad, I never felt like giving up. I simply adjusted and found ways to find peace within. I learned at a young age how to get things I wanted by collecting pop bottles and getting money for deposit and buying a cold bottle of Coke and chips. I would work at the local carnival when it was in town for a few dollars and cut grass for people or deliver newspapers. I worked all my life and had a little money in my pocket. I was an average boy who played with other kids and rode my bike through mud puddles. I was a free kid with no rules but also never had the urge to steal or cause trouble. Even to this day, I like all kind of things, like fishing and outdoor sports. I hid all my problems by joking around and finding funny people to hang around with.

I now have a wonderful wife who supports me in whatever I do, and I give her whatever she wants, provided we can afford it. I have a brand-new great-grandson named River Sage; his mother is Summer Rose. My other granddaughters are Brittny and Rebecca. My grandson is John and Kenny Jr. whom I have adopted and given him my last name, Eagle. I was picked up by a scout looking for Native Americans for a movie called *Big Sky*. My character is the chief's brother. I owe a lot to Rick Balentine who found me for the part. Rick is a well-known composer for TV and motion picture music. I went from nothing in this world to become a movie executive producer for Eagle Mehana films. Our first movie has won many awards and has been picked up by distribution company to market it worldwide. The company chooses Oscar short film that are Oscar qualified.

Since we were one of the finalists for selection, they contacted us. I have met many actors and actresses who became good friends of mine. One of my celebrity friends is Maurro Borelli, who is well-known in Hollywood, and we are working on a movie with him as I write. We have made three films at the moment and are doing very good. I was really excited to be asked to attend a big film festival in Las Vegas where we won two awards for our movie, *The Pride*. It was a first-class event where I had to wear a tux. I felt like a million dollars! I have also been at beautiful events in Chicago and made a lot of actor and beautiful actress friends. I learned that these are just people like everyone else, but they come alive behind a camera. I have learned so much about directing and producing movies that I normally do not like to discuss it with very many people because they would not understand and could get bored easily. I keep to myself and am kind of a recluse. I live in the country in Indiana and know a lot of people, including a lot of our law enforcement people. I support the local school nearby in Knox, Indiana, by attending football games and such. Filming movies is exciting and a real challenge.

My good friend and business partner, Edi Mehana, and I are as close as brothers, and I call him little brother. Edi Mehana and I met during the promotion of a western TV series called Big Sky, where we were both cast as lead actors. The movie is still in production. While I was in Chicago, we met and connected really good and became friends. Edi is an immigrant from Kosovo who went to school for acting and directing films. He left his entire family to come to America to peruse his dreams of being a director and actor. He went to the best college in Europe for this. He brought his wife and, to this day, has been waiting for ten years to become a citizen.

After a couple of years, one day Edi called me up and asked me if I would like to start a production company doing movies. At first I was intimidated and asked, "Why me? You know a lot of people in Chicago to do this, so why me?"

He replied, "You are the only man I trust."

At first I didn't understand, but as time went on I saw how some people will steel your script or simply just use you and give you no credit. One day he asked me to drive to Chicago to watch some short film being screened in a theater. It was mostly guests and directors with some local actors in the movies. I did not know it, but he was testing me to see what I thought about some of the work and acting. I watched two of the films and walked out of the theater. Edi was standing outside having a smoke and asked me what I thought. I told him right there and then!

If we can't do better than that? I am out and I mean it! He smiled and said exactly! I went on to tell him all the poor camera shots, acting lighting sound, and script. He then said you are correct. We will do way better than this. It was later that we got the script for our movie called The Pride. We bought our own cinema camera and hired professional people to do the camera work and sound and such. Edi did all the editing and had a friend help with the color and other tech parts. We went on and filmed it here at my home, on my property. We sent it in to many film festivals and won over twenty-five first place awards. We were also qualified for the Oscars but fell just short. We have gone on to do two other projects including A Gunman's Curse written by Ezekiel Martinez, who is a well-known screen writer in Hollywood. When Edi was the star and I played a Mexican/Indian outlaw called Laughing Jack Jim. It also has won many awards. We are currently working on a movie with another well-known director and friend named Mauro Borelli out of Hollywood. I have become like family to a lot of my acting friends, like Dominic Capone, who is a nephew of Al Capone. Dominic is cool.

As far as the hard times in life goes, this is my outlook: Every bad thing that happened in my life, I look at it as a lesson so that when I see a person going through a hard time, I know how they feel and have compassion and help them through it. I feel good when I help a person in need but also am wise enough to know those who are wanting something for nothing. I have seen women being abused by drunkard husbands while growing up. I hate men who abuse their innocent wives and got in to fights trying to help them. I do not allow liars in my circle or thieves or greedy, selfish people.

One of my favorite friends to chat with is Johnny Depp. It has taken me a long time to earn his trust, but I don't blame him because people have taken advantage of his kind spirit and caused him to be very careful with just anyone. He is not much of a talker and loves his music and reading. He is a really good musician and is in a big band called the Hollywood Vampires. He and I have not met up yet, but I feel it will happen soon. As for now, we just connect on Facebook. Life is only what we make of it. Our word is our bond. Without our word, we are nothing.

Many people know that about me. I try to be honest and kind, but I can also stand up for myself if needed. I normally don't cuss, but I can if I choose. Some people are so mean that they have caused me to do so. You see, sometimes when you are dealing with the devil, you have to speak his language in order for him to understand you.

So this is my life story—from the bottom ditches to being an award-winning film executive producer and actor. Never give up on your dreams no matter how old you get because life is not over until it's over.

ABOUT THE AUTHOR

Kenny Lone Eagle lives in the outskirts of Knox, Indiana in the country with his wife Linda and their German Shepherd dog Lady. He is an outdoorsman who loves and respects nature. He does not socialize with many but love people. The socializing distancing may stem from childhood. He has been given many talents by God such as building skills, memory recall, mechanics along with others. He enjoys helping others in need. Kenny seems to never have any cash in his wallet because if someone needs it he gives it to them. Although there is always room for improvement with the Almighty, he is a Christian. In the book he explains many times where He has been there for Mr. Eagle when he was in serious need. He hopes you enjoy this book it is as truthful as can be.